POCKET
GIRDLES

POCKET GIRDLES

and other
CONFESSIONS
of a NORTHWEST
FARMGIRL

by
MARIANNE LOVE

Greenhorn Mountain Press
Sandpoint, Idaho

Library of Congress Catalog Card Number: 94-76285

ISBN: 1-56044-293-X

Published by Greenhorn Mountain Press, Sandpoint, Idaho,
in cooperation with SkyHouse Publishers,
an imprint of Falcon® Publishing Co., Inc.,
Helena, Montana.

Editing by Mary Brown and SkyHouse Publishers.

Design, typesetting, and other prepress work by Falcon.

Cover painting and illustrations by Virginia Tibbs and Jim Tibbs.

Distributed by Falcon® Publishing Co., Inc., P. O. Box 1718, Helena,
Montana 59624. Phone 1-800-582-2665.

Manufactured in the United States of America

DEDICATIONS

To my mother and Harold,
for providing a remarkable childhood
and teaching my siblings and me what's important.

To my brothers and sisters—
Mike, Kevin, Barbara, Laurie, and Jim—
for the memories and their great appreciation for humor.

To my sister-in-law, Mary Brown,
who spent her summer editing the raw material.

To the students and faculty
at Sandpoint High School,
who have listened to these stories and laughed
during my twenty-five years of teaching.

To my friend Ann Gehring,
who has provided support by listening
to all of my latest creations over the telephone.
Her giggles got me through this.

To Patricia McManus Gass,
who gave me encouragment when I needed it,
and to her brother Patrick F. McManus, who inspired me.

To my own family—Bill, Willie, and Annie—
who have endured the ups and downs of this project.

Thanks to all of you.

TABLE *of* CONTENTS

Introduction: SAND CREEK PHENOMENON

For decades, something in the air around Sand Creek has caused bizarre behavior among adolescents living in the rural area north of Sandpoint, Idaho. It could be fumes rising from the hundreds of local cow pies that lurk among generous clumps of tall snake grass. The skunk cabbage that grows so abundantly in shaded areas along the stream bank might be emitting a mind-altering aroma. It could be the water.

SANDCREEK IN WINTER V. TIBBS '76

To date, researchers have not received adequate data for the big guns to come in and fully investigate this mysterious phenomenon. After reading my book, however, psychological experts may finally abandon the notion that earlier reports of nutty kids in the area were just isolated cases, or that true madness was restricted solely to famous humorist Patrick F. McManus.

In his popular writings about the outdoors, McManus tells of questionable childhood activities that occurred while he was growing up just a mile north of where I was reared. McManus lived on the east side of Sand Creek, which tumbles down its rock bed from Schweitzer Mountain, meanders through our beautiful resort community, and disappears into the vast blue-green waters of Lake Pend Oreille. Long after his childhood in the mid-1940s, youths caused or cooperated in activities beyond the realm of tolerated kid behavior near the spot.

I know this from personal experience.

As a victim of the behavior-disorienting malady during the 1950s and early 1960s, I now wish to make my data and personal observations public with the hope that researchers will feel compelled to get to the root of the problem. Over the years, this mysterious force has taken control of many angelic young minds in the Sand Creek vicinity, driving them to mischief serious enough to make their parents reconsider the pluses of China's zero-population movement. I hereby confess that I was one of the mind-altered kids, and so were my two older brothers, Mike and Kevin. Strangely enough, we now serve the world as "model citizens," as does Mr. McManus.

I ask readers for understanding and empathy as I unfold the facts of my youth. They have affected my psyche clear into adulthood; please do not judge. These revelations must be shared for the benefit of youngsters yet to come. If one child is spared the impish perversion that so dominated the formative years of McManus, my brothers, the neighborhood kids, and me, I shall not regret my disclosures.

Except for picky little details like the time of day an event may have occurred, or who REALLY was to blame, all information can be verified by documented evidence stored in my personal computer.

BLESS ME, FATHER, FOR I HAVE SINNED,

or, THE MAIL DOESN'T ALWAYS GO THROUGH

"Tell the father all your sins," Sister Ricardus advised us. "You should think about any times you've missed Mass or disobeyed your parents. Have you ever told a lie? Have you ever stolen anything?"

My body froze.

Unlike my classmates, who probably feared the darkness of the confessional more than the consequences of confessing, I held a burden deep within my soul that I dared not share with anyone, let alone God. My gut was churning, my palms sweating, and my pulse quickening, but I attempted to remain calm as my Catholic friends and I sat more attentive than we'd ever been in our young lives.

It was our third year of Sister School, and we occupied three pews at the rear of the church as St. Joseph's First Communion Class of 1955. As Sister Ricardus carefully ex-

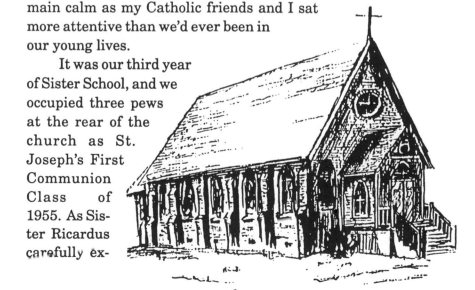

plained penance procedures, all of us dreaded our first encounter behind the doors at which we had curiously gawked so often. Sunday after Sunday I had watched with curiosity as little old ladies, their heads covered with scarves, entered the confessional with sober expressions then returned, clutching their rosaries, to their pews. I had never understood what they had been doing.

With Sister Ricardus's explanations, it began to make sense.

The dark, mysterious confessional has disappeared from St. Joseph's today. Our Catholic sense of guilt is different nowadays, too; back in the 1950s, sin seemed bigger and penance more intense. Young girls with heavy burdens on their souls had a tough time contemplating confession. There's still plenty of sin, but I don't feel as guilty as I did then—with one exception. That's the acknowledgment that I'm one of those "C and E" Catholics.

I first heard the term in the darkness of the confessional after whispering my most recent list of wrongdoings to Father O'Donovan, then our parish priest. I ended by saying, "I've missed Mass sixteen times."

He responded to my confession through the screen in his lyrical Irish brogue. "Now you don't waaaant to beeee a Ceeeeee and Eeeeee Caaatholiccc," he advised.

"Of course not, Father," I said, trying to recall all the words to the Act of Contrition. But I had no idea what he was talking about, so I checked with my sister Laurie, who had completed her confession just before mine. Laurie didn't know what "C and E" meant either. He hadn't mentioned it to her, so she must not have missed Mass quite so many times. Given the number of "Hail Marys" I'd been assigned for penance, we decided it must mean "cursed and evil."

Later I consulted with my friend Ann, who always seemed knowledgeable on church terminology. She told me that a "C and E" Catholic attends church only on Christmas and Easter. I felt insulted because I always showed up for Mass at least a dozen times a year, especially at the beginning of a new school year and fairly regularly after each dreaded confession.

Knowing the procedure and the proper prayer were the least of my worries; I knew the steps by heart and could recite the Act of Contrition to perfection. Sister Ricardus had prepared us well. What I couldn't do was tell our school's confessor, Father Dooley, all my sins. It was no problem to admit that I hadn't always honored my father and mother, and I knew he wouldn't be shocked to hear that I had initiated an occasional altercation with my older brothers. Even telling the truth about lying didn't pose a threat. But when Sister Ricardus posed, "Have you ever stolen anything?" I panicked.

"No, I can't tell THAT," I thought to myself. "I'll never tell anyone that—not even God! Sister said that God already knows everything; if He already does, why do I have to tell the priest the awful truth?"

That's what I dreaded about the confession business. As Sister Ricardus prepared us for our big moments in the booth, I remembered that sinful time eons ago when I was five. . . .

I never planned to commit a sin. My two older brothers and I had plenty of innocent activities to occupy our time on our forty-acre farm just north of the Bonner County Airport. Only eleven acres had been cleared at the time, so our wanderings beyond our yard included sorties into the spooky "deep woods" that extended for several acres along the west side of the place. Most of the time we played along the "cowboy" trails winding through the cedar trees in less threatening, more accessible woods just north of the house.

I seldom went to the deep woods alone because they scared me. A walk there represented a stab at independence, for which

I wasn't ready. A path dividing its midsection was the only part of the woods not like a jungle, so when I did have the nerve to walk through the area, I never strayed off the trail.

My brothers, Mike and Kevin, didn't encourage my exploration. When I ventured too near the "deep woods," they hunkered in the bushes a strategic ten feet past the opening of the trail, planning corrective activities. On good days, I entered the area, mustering up self confidence. I walked bravely, asserting that I would finally pass the milestone—"This time," I swore, "I'll march all the way down the trail." Or so I thought.

Five seconds later, the loudest, most ferocious growl ever heard roared through the forest.

Ten seconds later, I was back on the front porch, hair standing on end, eyes wide as saucers, with shivers shaking my entire body.

Fifteen seconds later, two brothers ambled across the front yard, sporting malicious grins at having destroyed my confidence for another year.

Never satisfied with such simple harassment, they prolonged my misery with snatches from literary classics of their learned backgrounds, which in addition to *Goldilocks and the Three Bears* included *Alice in Wonderland*, from which their favorite line came. "Marianne's madder than a hatter," the muted chorus began.

My preliminary reaction was always the same. "Pretend you don't hear it," I coached myself, maintaining an expressionless demeanor and seemingly ignoring their presence while scrawling pictures in the dirt. The first ten soft repetitions hardly ruffled me. But my tormentors came nearer, methodically increasing the volume like a troupe of cheerleaders.

"Marianne's madder than A HATTER . . . Marianne's madder THAN A HATTER . . . Marianne's MADDER THAN A HATTER . . . MARIANNE'S MADDER THAN A HATTER . . . MARIANNE'S . . . "

I could stand no more! Launching myself from the porch, I tried to escape to the back yard, seeking relief from the interminable chants of the fiends. My exit served as a sign that success was imminent. Following a safe six feet behind, my brothers continued their chorus.

"MARIANNE'S MADDER THAN A HATTER . . . "

Primitive instincts set in. I had to retaliate. Instead of my usual guttural grunts (characteristic of all Brown children), I squawked out a loud, piercing "EEEEAHHHHH!" I cannot effectively trace the origin of this utterance. My only clue is that it must be vocal residue from one of my past lives—possibly during the Paleozoic Era.

Meanwhile, inside the house, my mother might be writing letters and listening to her favorite radio soap opera, *Ma Perkins.* Her peace and quiet came to an abrupt end. "MARIANNE'S MADDER THAN A HATTER . . . EEEAHHH . . . MARIANNE'S MADDER THAN A HATTER . . . EEEAHHH. . . MARIANNE'S MADDER THAN A HATTER . . . EEEAHHH!"

And *she* could stand no more!

The back door flew open. Standing on the porch with hands planted on her hips, she shouted, "Marianne, that's enough of the God-awful noise! Get in this house and go to your room!"

Such harassment drove me to a life of crime at the tender age of five. One criminal option could have been the murder of the malevolent brothers, but I lacked the scientific knowledge to poison the peanut butter they glopped onto slices of bread stolen whenever our parents left the house. Instead I decided to mimic their talents for being sneaky thieves.

That was how my sin originated.

Seeking refuge in the woods from my daily torments, I discovered twelve mailboxes on a single stand across the roadside ditch from our fence. These boxes served some of the other families, few as they were, on Route #1 at the north end of Boyer. The collection of containers interested me. After cantering through the trees to them on my dependable stick horse, I hollered, "Whoa!" and dropped Stickie behind a stump. Then I watched as a light blue station wagon pulled up—our mailman, Bill Brockus.

Crouching behind a drooping cedar limb, I silently spied as Bill opened a box, shoved something in, slapped it shut, and moved his Rambler forward, repeating the process several times. Unaware of the pair of brown eyes peering at him, he masterfully carried out his duty. Soon he finished, and the Rambler's idling grew to a medium roar as it rounded the corner on Boyer, heading south.

I was fascinated by what I had seen, since I had precious little opportunity to fill or empty our own mailbox. My brothers guarded its access; there was daily warfare between them to determine who got the honor of carrying the mail to the house. Usually a sprint to the road, along with some tripping and slugging, determined who would be the victor. Bullied anyway, I never considered entering the daily competition. Each morning, when the boys perched in their starting positions, contemplating effective dirty tricks to wipe each other out, my existence held no importance to them.

But my wonderful new discovery in a far corner of the woods opened some great solo possibilities, which could be perfectly timed with their great mail races. While they were so engrossed, I could disappear and make my way north on Stickie to my new postal gold mine. There, I had no competition and great odds—one for twelve instead of two for one. I could empty twelve boxes, open all the letters myself, and keep them in the woods near our pretend "fort," a collection of hollow logs. The soft underbrush and cushiony white pine needles made it an ideal place for a make-believe post office.

I acted on my fantasy the very next day. As anticipated, Mike and Kevin began plotting individual strategies for reaching our mailbox first. As they did so, I scurried from view around the corner of the house, riding Stickie to my hiding spot. The forenoon sun shone down through the cedar branches, and I soon heard a car roll to a stop in front of the boxes.

Feeling a bit anxious that first day, I waited to make sure Bill was long gone before daring to leave the woods. I also remembered the adage "look both ways" before climbing out of the ditch beside the road. Once the path was clear, I quickly opened each container, unloaded the contents that Bill had just stuffed within, and piled them in my arms. The entire process went much more quickly than Bill's depositing because I didn't have to drive a car. Within a minute or so I had scrambled back across the ditch and carefully crawled through the barbed wire fence, trying not to drop any of my booty. A few letters fell to the ground, but I didn't care too much. My pile still exceeded anything the boys were fighting over at the house.

To ensure that no one discovered my newly found form of recreation, I selected a soft spot in an old stump as a depository for the stolen goods. After sorting through the array of envelopes and pretending to read the important contents, I dug a substantial hole, by hand, near the stump. Then I buried the letters, mounted my horse and, with a rare feeling of superiority, headed back to the house for sandwiches.

Besides enriching my mind through all the "reading," my new activity provided the answer to many problems. For a short time each day I avoided my big bully brothers and experienced a true feeling of accomplishment. Moreover, I developed the talents of cunning, careful planning, and concealment. I also felt independent and a bit smug because for once I had outsmarted the boys.

As the days passed, Bill faithfully brought a healthy armful of mail for me to sort through within the safety of the woods. Occasionally he would attach a parcel to someone's mailbox. One in particular was memorable—a sizable package attached to Lucille and John Hudon's box. I had to throw the brown parcel into the woods, because it was too cumbersome to crawl through the barbed wire with it in hand. Once I arrived at my hiding spot, my fingers went wild trying to rip the stubborn cardboard open. My frantic efforts were rewarded, since I discovered within its white, tissue-paper stuffing at least a dozen pairs of colored nylons in bright blues, yellows, reds, and greens. Like a princess performing before her court, I wrapped these around my neck as scarves. As my fascination with these colored treasures wore off, I realized they were indeed hot items. Burying them along with the rest of my stash seemed unwise; I needed to remove them from my territory. The best thing to do was the obvious. Strewing the nylons along the ditch and leaving the box in full view of the road, I rationalized that whoever discovered them would surely suspect a bear had ripped the box off the mailbox. Yeah! Right! That was a plausible story. After so disposing of the evidence, I left the wooded area feeling self-assured.

I can't recall exactly how long this thievery took place. No one had seen me going about my daily postal duties—or so I thought. The only time I got really nervous was the time that Mother returned from a horseback ride on her saddle bred mare Largo. After putting Largo up, she came into the house dressed in her baggy jodhpurs and sporting a crop in her right hand. Upon entering the living room, she inquired, "Do you know anything about those colored nylons scattered along the ditch on the back road, Marianne?"

With the calm demeanor of a seasoned liar, I coolly responded, "Colored nylons? No. Where are they on the back road?" My reaction was so artificial that it alone should have given me away. One look at her skeptical face told me that Mother, in fact, didn't believe me. She interrogated further. I remained cool, issuing further denials.

She finally dropped the subject and headed toward her bedroom to change. Once she was out of sight, I gasped for breath, thinking how close that call had been. Nevertheless, the next day I marched off through the woods once more to gather and file my envelopes. I thought of myself as an unofficial postal worker, sorting letters and burying them in my cache.

Folks along North Boyer were puzzled about the mail situation. Some wondered why their paychecks had failed to arrive. Others hadn't received their monthly bills. The neighbors had been conferring and comparing notes. I was a pretty smooth mail thief, except for one oversight—Mrs. Moore. Mrs. Moore lived on the corner opposite the mailbox row. Since her house was partially hidden behind some big white pine trees, I thought she couldn't see in my direction. That false assumption led to my downfall. She did look out her window, and she could see more than just pine trees. One day she spotted me on my unappointed rounds and notified the authorities.

A few days later a car rolled into our driveway, and two men dressed in suits stepped out. I was the only one in the yard at the time, so they politely asked if my parents were home. Since they were so nice and seemed so official, I wasted no time guiding them to the house. They said they wanted to talk to my folks in private, so immediately after introducing them I left, entirely unaware of my approaching fate. I was sitting on the back porch when Mother summoned me.

"These men would like to ask you some questions, Marianne," she said, with a pleasant smile. The genial atmosphere and feeling of warmth made me relaxed and eager to talk.

"We've had some problems with the mailboxes down the road," one of the visitors said, "and we heard that you may know something about the missing mail. Could you possibly tell us what happened to it?"

I was flattered that the polite, friendly gentleman seemed so genuinely interested in me. His professional manner made me feel that my responses would be considered very important.

"Yes," I replied.

"Did you take any of the mail?" he asked.

"Yes."

"What did you do with the mail?" he gently continued. He had lured me into his confidence. I told the whole story, without skipping a detail about my post office job and my underground cache inside the woods.

After a brief lecture about how important it was for people to receive their mail and a gentle request that I stay away from the mailboxes from now on, the gentlemen shook hands with my parents, said a friendly good-bye, and drove away.

For me, the visit began and ended all too quickly. That was the first time in my life I had felt so official and so important. As a country kid, I seldom saw a suit; having two well-dressed, distinguished gentlemen from some big city show up wishing to speak with me boosted my child's ego. For one brief, shining moment, I was overcome with pride.

My Camelot was all too brief.

What happened next left an indelible impression on me clear through the rest of my childhood, adolescence, and young adult years. My parents' split-second transformation from cordiality to absolute rage was memorable. The subsequent spanking I received for my violation was understandable. My mother's revelation that those men in suits were postal inspectors from the federal government and her further revelation that I now had a criminal record disordered my normally carefree state. My conscience went into overdrive. I knew my soul was the blackest of black. I knew I was beyond bad, and I knew that everybody else knew too. I figured my crime was going to be a front-page story in the *Sandpoint News Bulletin*. No longer could

I face society with a smile. Crowds would glare as I endured public censure as North Boyer's notorious mail thief.

"Marianne?" Sister Ricardus announced. My glazed, distant expression revealed that something was amiss, but I quickly composed myself enough to convince her that I was really just daydreaming.

"Say the Act of Contrition," she ordered, obviously miffed that I hadn't been paying absolute attention to her carefully organized, important instructions. Nevertheless, the perfection with which I breezed through the prayer redeemed me enough to elicit a pleased smile from the nun when I finished.

I sat rigidly awaiting my turn, expending little energy on my favorite pastime—watching others. For once, I couldn't care less; I ignored my classmates as each marched into the booth, announced a lifetime of sins, stumbled through the "Act of Contrition," received the blessing, left the room, and returned to their pews to offer prayers of penance.

Paramount in my conscience at the time was just how badly God would treat me if I happened to forget to mention the mail incident. Conveniently forgetting on purpose seemed my only choice. Besides, I could always catch it later in another confession and probably do a better job telling the story. "If I haven't told it by now and God hasn't done anything, maybe He will just look forward to hearing about it later," I reasoned. He could wait.

And wait He has, for more than thirty years. Just as I couldn't muster the courage that June day in 1955, I have turned coward during every confession since. Every time I've set foot inside that booth or sat before the priest in more recent times, I've cleared my conscience by pointing out my other infractions—lying a time or two, or letting a little earthy language slip from the tongue now and then. I've also confessed my moments of anger and my tendency to be "uncharitable," as my mother terms gossip. Not once in all the intervening years, however, have I unloaded the burden of the postal pilfering to a priest.

That's why I've taken the time to write about it. Upon reading this public declaration of my unpardonable sin, some forgiving priest may just find it within his heart to broach the subject in one of my upcoming confessions. Now that I have spit out my sins face-to-face, I'm hoping this kind man will recognize me and say, "Oh, you're the one, aren't you? The one who stole the North Boyer mail in 1953?"

A quick "yes" and finally I'll receive forgiveness.

How about it, Father? Hasn't the confessional statute of limitations run out?

THE GREAT
PENCIL MYSTERY
and Other MATERNAL
CHALLENGES

I've been known to express my opinion occasionally.

I don't know why I have this quality, except that experts on the subject have told me, "When you grow up, you become your mother." If that's true, I understand completely why I might be a bit opinionated and inclined to speak up for my beliefs.

I had a good mentor.

Mother's influence has been paramount to my siblings and me. I admire her more than any person I have ever known because of her strength of character, courage, talent, and incurable sense of humor. She has always hated quitters, making it clear she allows no room in her life for anyone who dares to be one. She's the ubiquitous conscience that has pushed me through some of my more difficult times. Packaged in a five-foot, two and one-half-inch frame, she has never let her short stature get in the way of righting her children's wrongs . . . or the sins of anyone else

who chooses to err in her presence. An entire squad of young-sters and their parents learned that firsthand one day at the Bonner County Fairgrounds.

After several years as a 4-H horse leader, Mother became a familiar fixture at the annual county-wide shows. She knew all the rules and worked overtime to see that they were enforced to the letter. One year in the early 1980s, she served as gate stew-ard at the 4-H show. As youngsters lined up with their steeds for upcoming classes, she thoroughly checked each exhibitor's number, tack, clothing, and attitude to see that all were up to snuff.

Most kids sensed the need to act appropriately. However, about midway through the day, a rebellious bareback rider—not a 4-H member, of course—brought chaos to Mother's orga-nized domain by racing through the line-up, scattering kids, parents, and horses. As he turned and started galloping back through the warm-up area, Mother intercepted him.

"Get that horse out of here and stay out!" she yelled.

He left—for about ten minutes. Then he came charging through the mass with more reckless abandon than he had in his initial performance. Once again, with clipboard in hand, she chased him down.

"I *said*, 'Get that horse out of here and don't come back',"
she repeated, enunciating each word with ample volume for any slightly deaf kid to comprehend. Glaring at her, the renegade begrudgingly directed his mount away once more. But the young demon decided to charge the 4-H troops one more time and make it clear to the bossy woman that no one was going to tell *him* what to do. Full speed ahead, he cleared the ranks of the warm-up arena.

Mother wouldn't have it.

Marching toward him once more, she eyed him and yelled at the top of her lungs, "GET THAT HORSE OUT OF HERE

AND DON'T COME BACK! I'll have you removed from the grounds!"

The incorrigible kid stopped his mount, got off, pulled the lathered-up horse behind him, and walked straight to where Mother stood. Once there, he looked her straight in the face and shot daggers into her eyes with the silent rage of a serial killer.

Mother stood her ground and glared upward at the kid, who towered over her by about six inches. The awestruck crowd remained motionless as they watched the stand-off.

"DROP DEAD, B-I-T-C-H!!" the invader commanded.

Silence. No one moved. Mother eyed him back in a stand-off reflective of the famous photo of the lone Chinese student resisting a huge military tank in Tiananmen Square.

"I W-I-L-L NOT!!" she barked back.

The dumbfounded kid didn't know what to do. There was nothing left for him but a silent retreat in total disgrace—this time permanently as the fairgrounds caretaker escorted him from the arena. The stare-down at the fairgrounds corral was talked about for days afterward.

Nobody ever got off easy with this lady if they intended to cheat, steal, lie, or break the rules of society—least of all her children. We learned that lesson well once with an unusual prop: a yellow pencil.

"All right! Who carved on this pencil?"

We were lounging around in our bedrooms one day in the mid-1950s when Mother's irritated voice jolted us to attention.

"Who did it?" she barked again.

Silence.

"You kids get out here right now!"

A minute later her pre-adolescent darlings Mike, Kevin, and Marianne (ages eleven, nine, and eight, respectively) stood rank-and-file in the living room while Sergeant Tibbs resumed interrogation.

"Which one of you did this?" Glaring and huffing, she brandished a yellow No. 2 pencil in her right hand, appearing to have a nervous twitch as she shook the writing tool up and down.

Three pairs of seemingly innocent eyes followed the path of the twitching pencil.

"Somebody carved on this pencil. Look at it." She held the pencil still for a moment and pointed at a minute spot about one-fourth inch long near the eraser. Sure enough, someone had carved on it, removing about one-millionth of an ounce of paint. The pencil was scarred for life.

We all stood mute.

"All I want to know is who carved on it," she demanded.

"I didn't," Mike said.

"I didn't," Kevin followed.

"I didn't," I said, concluding the denial line-up.

"Someone carved on this pencil sometime today, because I used it this morning and the paint was still there," she announced.

Mother was a formidable, even militant disciplinarian. She also thought she was related to Sherlock Holmes. Detection and observation were crucial if she were to survive her herd of precocious kids; she had fought too many losing battles in her effort to keep food in the cupboards for nightly meals, and she had been dumbfounded and totally embarrassed when federal postal authorities happened on the scene one day to talk to her mail-stealing daughter. For her own sanity and basic survival, she knew she must keep close track of our every move. Mother's eye for detail became sharper by the day, and the pencil incident showed she had graduated from a hawk to an eagle.

"You might as well admit it," she urged.

"I didn't."

"It wasn't me."

"I didn't carve on any pencil."

Mother not only had a full-fledged pencil desecrator in the house but also a liar. This thoroughly incensed her and drove her to drastic means of punishment. "Okay," she said. "No TV until someone admits it."

I gulped. "No, no, she couldn't do that to us!" I thought. We had just adapted to *having* to watch television shows every night. It had taken some doing, but now I rather liked watching *The Line-up*, *Cheyenne*, and *Gunsmoke*.

"From now until someone tells the truth, you'll all go to your bedrooms every night after dinner," she instructed. "You will shut your doors and not watch TV. I'll not have any liars around this house."

Since no one volunteered any information, we went our separate ways.

"That's not fair," I said to myself, seated near the front porch, my head between my knees as I poked at the dirt with a twig from the lilac bush. "I didn't do it. Why should I have to miss my TV? One of those slobs did it. Now we all have to suffer." My argument was well-organized, and I continued to agree with myself, uttering several "Yeah!"s while dreading the evening alone. My bedroom was located just off the living room, not more than ten feet from the television set. To make matters worse, its door closed the wrong direction for me to be able to sneak any peeks while Mother and Harold sat out there enjoying the evening's programs.

When we had eaten our dinner and finished dessert, Mother held another inquiry. "Did anyone carve on the pencil?" she asked.

Not a sound. Our futures looked dismal.

"Okay, get to your rooms," she ordered. Mike and Kevin headed for their bedroom, which was just off the kitchen. They would not hear the TV, so would not be tempted by the programs like I would. Furthermore, they had not been sentenced to solitary confinement. What was even worse yet, one of them was a guilty pencil-carver, and he wasn't 'fessing up.

I trudged to my bedroom, uttering "dirtyrackapracks" all the way. It was going to be a long, boring evening, and I wasn't even guilty. Life was unjust.

That first night was agony. Mother and Harold remained at the table chatting and smoking cigarettes. I slumped around in my room, trying to while away the time with anything that would take my mind off what I'd soon be missing in the living room. Drawing horse tails on my tablet kept me busy for about five minutes. I lay on the bed and counted the knots on the pine ceiling. I got desperate and started folding the clothes in one of my dresser drawers.

Through the door I heard my parents retire to the living room, then the click of the television power button. Walt Disney was introducing this week's show from Frontierland, *The Adventures of Davy Crockett*. I was sick. We loved westerns, and Davy Crockett and Mike Fink were hot stuff at the time. We had to sit in our rooms and miss it.

I hated that pencil and loathed the deceitful brother. Standing and resting my face on fisted hands, I started making dirty faces into the mirror on my dresser. Then I made more silent commentary. "I hate them. Why do I have to suffer when they did it?" I asked myself. Such solo reasoning provided no satisfaction. I plopped on the bed; bundling myself under the covers so I couldn't hear the TV, I eventually drifted off to sleep.

I awoke the next morning in an ugly mood. We all grouched around the house until lunch, when Mother lined us up again for the daily inquisition. "Does anyone have anything to tell me?" she asked.

Again, nothing. And no suspended sentence. We would have to spend another endless evening in our rooms until somebody told the truth.

The second night of life behind the door with no TV was just as bad as the first. I tried to figure some way to prop the door open a notch so I could peek through the crack. The folks kept a close watch, however, and any hint of door movement met with immediate reaction.

"Marianne, what are you doing in there? Would you leave your door shut, please?"

The third day came. No confession. No TV. I became so desperate that night when Clint Walker as "Cheyenne" came on the tube that I even considered an insane plan to end the siege.

"All right. I did it. I carved on the pencil," I envisioned blurting out. "I'm really sorry and I'll never do it again if you'll just let me come out and watch this program." Behind the door, I practiced mouthing the confession, but somehow sanity prevailed. It did not make sense to lie about something I didn't do when she was mad because someone had lied about what they had done. "Yeah, that would be stupid," I thought, keeping quiet and drifting off into another miserable slumber.

The next day brought a break in the case. Mother had picked up the pencil from the living room dresser and found new evidence. Sometime during the twenty-four-hour period a person with the initial "K" had added his mark. We were summoned to the living room.

"I've solved the mystery," Mother announced. "Kevin, why didn't you admit it? You carved on the pencil, didn't you?"

"No, I didn't," he said.

"Yes, you did. There's a 'K' added to the carving."

"But I didn't do it," he insisted. "I've never touched that pencil. I didn't do it."

Mother was incensed. "Why are you lying?" she continued. "Admit it! You carved on the pencil!"

"I didn't do it!" Kevin stood his ground.

Mother moved in for the kill. She would make an example

out of Kevin. "Nobody watches TV until somebody admits carving on the pencil," she declared.

We stomped out of the room and out of the house, gathering under one of the white pine trees in the front yard, where a heated discussion ensued. I complained because I couldn't watch my programs. Kevin complained because he was getting the blame. Kevin got the blame a lot of times—mainly because, of the three of us, he was the biggest imp. Mike didn't have much to say. We were all mad at each other, and we were all mad at Mother and Harold. Mother and Harold were mad at the unknown liar, and as long as they didn't know which one of us that happened to be, we would all suffer.

It was beginning to look as if we wouldn't be able to watch TV again until we reached adulthood, when the siege suddenly ended. The TV ban was off. It all happened so fast I hardly knew the details. Mother had gotten the confession she wanted.

Mike had been the culprit. He had inflicted the wound on the pencil, never thinking it would be a big deal until Mother made it so. Aware of her wrath, he decided to stay mum, but his bad decision worsened as the week wore on. He sensed anger growing among family members and decided to pass on the guilt by trying to implicate Kevin with the initial 'K' on the pencil. When Kevin wouldn't stray from his denial, Mike decided to throw in the towel and finally admit his crime.

Mother waited until this disclosure to inform us that she really didn't give a hoot about the pencil blemish. She just didn't want liars in the house. It was a good early lesson for Mike because he later attended the United States Military Academy at West Point and never once abused the academy's sacred honor code. Kevin gained back some credibility he may have lost through earlier in-house crimes. As for me, from that day forward, every time I have been tempted to tell a whopper, a big yellow pencil has popped into my mind. The threat of TV deprivation has kept me honest.

Mother taught us values and life skills through the example she set. In disciplining us, she used techniques that would prove useful to us in later life. One of the skills I learned from her came from our favorite rainy-day pastime in my childhood years.

There was no formal announcement. The moments just happened in front of our medicine cabinet mirror. One of us might be combing her hair there when the other slipped into the bathroom. Seconds later, we'd be giggling our heads off "out-facing" each other. The object was to contort our countenances into the most grotesque, ghoulish shapes possible. Sometimes we competed to see who could stretch her tongue the farthest around the point and bridge of her nose. Mother usually won this because of her generously sized "purebred" nose. We often spent ten to fifteen minutes amusing ourselves before leaving the bathroom, wiping tears from our eyes and clearing our throats with the hysterical glee.

Mother introduced me to this form of pseudo-narcissistic behavior after what had to be years of practice. I knew she had perfected the craft of facial weaponry because she could unload her arsenal on me at a second's notice. Although she would do things with her face to make me laugh, Mother was equally talented at making the toughest thug cringe in horror. Her specialty was known as the "hate stare."

I can remember perfectly nice mornings when I tagged along with Mother at Chapman's Food Market on First Avenue as she shopped for the week's groceries. While she strolled down the hardwood aisles selecting sacks of flour, sugar, cans of veggies, and other necessities, I babbled incessantly. "Can we have some candy? I'll push the cart. Oh, let's buy some Hershey bars. Are ya gonna get some cookies? Oh, yuck, I hate tongue spread."

Mother never appreciated my shopping advice; she could take it just so long. Suddenly the shopping cart would come to an abrupt halt. Gripping the handle, she would wheel her upper body around, freeze into position, and shoot me the most spiteful, hate-filled glare ever conceived by humankind.

Pierced by the electric, intense, laserlike eye shots, I usually cringed like a wounded puppy and cut the yapping immediately. The rest of the shopping venture was bliss for her and total misery for me.

Mother's hate stare had such an impact on me that, years later, after taking a job as a high school teacher, I spent months practicing my own evil eye in front of my bathroom mirror. It has been an effective weapon in my classroom ever since.

As I approach my half-century mark, and as my mother defies the institutional attitudes of those in their seventies, her maternal influence still drives me. My admiration of her, my respect for the job she has done as a mother, and occasional fear of her disapproval keep me in line . . . most of the time.

INSTANT KIDS:
Did HAROLD *Pass the* FATHERHOOD TEST?

"It was pretty scary. And it sure wasn't easy either. But you kids turned out pretty good."

Over the years, Harold has often assessed the experience of acquiring an instant family of four with a blend of pride and relief. After all, he was a thirty-eight-year-old, lifelong bachelor when he and Mother got married in March of 1954. They went on a honeymoon to Polson and Troy, Montana, after exchanging wedding vows in Thompson Falls. The newlyweds drove around the western half of the state taking about four hundred slides of white-tailed and mule deer that blended perfectly with the gray winter surroundings. That honeymoon slide collection kept us occupied for hours at future living room showings, as we all had a great time playing "Find the Deer."

"There it is! I see it!" Kevin jumped up and ran toward the screen. "See, it's peeking out from behind the bush." Placing his index finger on a muddy brown blob amidst the winter brush, he finally convinced the living room skeptics that he really

Virginia [signature]
1994

had spotted a deer, proving that Harold hadn't foolishly wasted Kodak film.

Our new dad was an outdoorsman and a cowboy who had ridden forty thousand acres of range in the mountains of Montana's Madison Valley. He walked with a limp because of a logging accident years before, when a team of horses had run away with him. Before marrying Mother, he had lived down the road at the Racicots', where he kept his Appaloosa stallion named Toby. A shared love for horses attracted him to Mother, but along with her came three half-grown kids. Harold didn't seem to mind. If he had fears, he didn't show them as he assumed his job as a father.

Soon after they were married, the kitchen table became the family center. Mother fixed three ample meals a day. Breakfast always included cereal, toast, and homemade jams. Harold milked Bossy night and morning, so he enjoyed the bounties of that chore with his meal. Each morning he poured thick cream over his Wheaties breakfast cereal and loaded six to eight teaspoons of sugar on top. My brothers watched his routine and soon followed suit. After sumptuous dinners of beef, potatoes, veggies, tossed green salads, and freshly prepared desserts, we sat for at least an hour around the table discussing the day's events and making plans for what we'd be doing to improve our family farm.

When Harold first came he set about clearing more land to expand the farming operation. Once stump piles were burned and cleared away, he plowed, disked, and harrowed the fields in preparation for planting. Then the whole family spent days picking up sticks, an activity that was meant to demonstrate Harold's calm, logical approach to work.

We had 3,056,219 sticks to pick up in a six-acre field designated for hay. Harold hooked the hay wagon to the back of his Ford tractor, and the entire family rode out to the field. Mother brought along a thermos of Kool-Aid to quench our thirst during this fruitful day of blood, sweat, and sticks. Parents smiled, thinking, "This is the life." Kids learned the value of a good day's toil.

On stick-picking days, all went well for the first fifteen minutes or so. That was about as long as Mike and Kevin could manage to work side-by-side without something setting them off—Kevin getting to one of Mike's sticks first, for instance. The minor incident led to inefficient loading of items onto a farm vehicle. As the boys walked beside the wagon and stooped down to scoop up the stick crop, the temperature and their tempers soared simultaneously. With glares and unkind remarks, they released their frustration by hurling handfuls of sticks . . . aimed just off-target from the wagon but with bull's-eye accuracy on each other.

The action got better by the minute. Sticks flew. Insults increased. Parents yelled. Family bonding suffered. Harold's disgust at the failure of his plan to clear the field harmoniously eventually engendered a plan to teach these boys how to rid themselves of antagonistic feelings.

He bought some boxing gloves.

As an enthusiastic fan of the *Saturday Night Fights*, Harold borrowed the idea, figuring Mike and Kevin ought to resolve their differences in a controlled atmosphere rather than out in the field where God and all the neighbors could see (and hear) them trying to kill each other. Whenever their sibling anger got too aggressive, the boys were sent to the box stall in the barn. They stood in opposite corners until Harold laced up their gloves then let them go at it. They could pound each other's snouts, and Harold could not only referee but also enjoy an amateur version of his favorite TV show.

The plan worked for a while, but not in the long run. Years later, during haying season, Mother encountered battles simi-

27

lar to the stick episode as she drove the flatbed around the field while Mike and Kevin loaded bales of hay several tiers high. Something about work, hot weather, and the out-of-doors brought out the worst sibling rivalry, and Harold's Release Aggression Through Boxing plan never quite cured their tendency to throw things at each other. The projectiles changed into sixty-pound bales, flung from one brother on the ground toward the other standing on a seven-foot-high load.

Doubling as chauffeur and referee, Mother's tolerance for the hay field war did not last long. Yelling at them and demanding that they stop rarely proved effective. When she couldn't take it any longer, Mother launched her offensive: slamming on the brakes, dumping several bales and maybe even a teenage boy in the process, all of which had to be reloaded. Fighting stopped and brother bonding began.

Except for the occasional family feuds in the fields, we really did love farming because we got to ride on the wagons or in the tractor loader. Anytime Harold started his equipment, he could count on a kid showing up to beg for a ride. Even if it was just a ride across the barnyard, we were willing to wait for the chance to climb aboard. We especially loved it when Harold raised us up and down in the loader.

With the farm, life took on new meaning and a greater sense of order. We were each assigned daily chores. Mine were to dust, set the table, and dry the dishes every day, and to clean the bathroom on Saturday. The boys did the outside chores. We were expected to do our work without being reminded. And it had to pass inspection; if it didn't, we had to do it over.

We also got to know Harold's cows. Donna and Mystic, the herd's ringleaders, demanded the most attention. They loved being scratched and would follow us across the field for a free back rub. In 1955 Harold bought a herd bull from Merle Griffith, who lived in Priest River. From that point on we looked forward to early spring, when slimy, little, white-faced calves arrived, staggered around, and, within hours, transformed into adorable, cuddly, brown-and-white cotton balls bouncing and tearing across the fields.

I loved those days of expectation during calving season. Many times I jumped out of bed with the early light of day, sneaking out in hope of being the first to spot a new calf. Whenever a new baby appeared, I first checked to see if it was a "he" or a "she," then high-tailed it for the house to awaken Mother and Harold with the news. Within minutes, Harold was dressed in his jeans, shirt, boots, and hat. Never one to get too excited, he calmly ambled out to wherever the cow had chosen to give birth and checked the calf to see that everything was all right. Harold's calm demeanor complemented Mother's intensity in matters of parenting.

That became evident soon after they were married, when we kids attended Sister School. Sister School was held for two weeks after public school let out, when three or four nuns from Immaculate Heart of Mary Academy in Coeur d'Alene came to give us the full dose of the religious education we were missing by not attending Catholic schools. The nuns meant well, but Sister School was not exactly every child's favorite activity, especially since it came immediately after nine months of public school. It was especially disconcerting because our non-Catholic friends were free to ride their bicycles past St. Joseph's on the way to City Beach while we were forced to suffer through six hours a day in hot classrooms, learning more of the Baltimore Catechism and memorizing The Apostle's Creed. The Sister School experience created long-lasting friendships, however, among the Catholic kids of Sandpoint. Like soldiers at war, we endured and bonded.

Most of us.

Occasionally, some youngsters had heard enough about sin

to help them decide to get some hands-on experience—ditching Sister School. Sean Garvey and my brother Kevin were in the second grade group when they skipped out right as class was beginning one morning. Kevin had a hole in the seat of his pants, and Sean just plain didn't want to be there.

The two were missing for the entire day. When they didn't show up at the end of classes, parents were alerted. The adults got serious and called the police. Search parties scoured the town, and telephones rang as concerned parties compared notes on where the two runaways might have gone. The search finally ended about 7 P.M. when the boys gave up hiding under the bleachers at the sale yard on Oak Street, about four blocks west of the church. Both were taken home to face their relieved but disgusted families.

They also faced a guilt trip the next morning from Sister Ricardus, who grabbed her chance to set us all straight. She had charm and charisma that endeared her to us, and she seemed fully aware that her every word captivated even the most idle of minds. Lecturing those boys was intended to be a lesson for all children who might be tempted to err during future days of the summer religious program. "You should be ashamed," she told them as the entire Sister School population sat, silently as statues, in the church pews. "You need to consider someone besides yourselves. You, Kevin, think of what you did to your little sister, leaving her here all alone," she continued. "God is certainly not happy with you today."

Somehow I didn't think I'd really suffered much in Kevin's absence, but bringing my helplessness into the lecture seemed to serve Sister Ricardus's purpose.

Harold's approach that night contrasted dramatically with the scathing spiel we had heard from Sister Ricardus. As Mother sat at the table, smoking and restraining her wrath, Harold did all the talking. "Now, we'd like you kids to let us know whenever you plan to go someplace," he said calmly. "That way we won't have to worry about where you are." Harold wasted few words in letting us know what he expected, and he delivered them in such a way that any self-respecting kid would feel terrible if he or she ever broke his trust.

Subtle but effective dinner table lectures were Harold's trademark whenever something—or someone—had gone wrong. Many times he managed damage control, after which he assessed the situation and discussed the behavior he wanted to see in the future.

Harold was tested again less than a year later when we set a stump in the woods on fire in mid-winter. Kevin had shown me how to ignite an entire book of matches at once, and I had been perfecting the technique one day in the woods, also practicing using the matchbook torch to ignite some newspaper that just happened to be at my side. The stump could not resist the flames and soon caught fire. It smoldered for days afterward but, in spite of the worry I caused him, Harold reacted with the same calm approach he had had after Kevin's Sister School fiasco. Both Kevin and I received another talking to, this time about the dangers of playing with matches and the need to refrain from such activity in the future.

Years passed, full of slide shows, family drives, sibling disputes, count-the-deer contests, and dozens of baby calves. We three provided our stepfather with a rigorous training ground, but Harold survived fatherhood. We always figured he did a pretty fair job. And apparently we passed his test, for he liked his role enough to become a father three more times. Those later kids turned out pretty good, too.

THE *Used* CAR, *Abused* CAR BLUES

We Loves are not the typical American family.

We do come close. There are two of us—one male and one female—who play parents. We have two kids. We also have two dogs.

We have FOUR cars.

Before anyone gets the idea that we're related to the Rockefellers or the Gettys, meet our automotive lot. Our 1976 brown Buick Century has to be pushed around the driveway by hand. Our 1979 Ford 4-x-4 pickup truck is great fun when it's time to turn, since its signals, when they choose to work, do so only by hand. And I probably won't have the hands to operate the aforementioned vehicles much longer if I keep driving our 1989 Dodge Caravan. (Here's a likely scenario: I'm driving down Highway 95. The van, without prompting, takes its habitual turn into Yoke's Pac 'N Save at the Bonner Mall. Just as it leaves the highway, the left door, which has been sprung and flashing the red "door ajar" light for three years, decides it's time to fall off. Since I don't wear seat belts in local traffic, I fall out onto the pavement, where a Pizza Hut delivery man in a rush drives over my left arm, severing it with his Subaru Brat. Blood flies, and some lucky pizza lovers find an extra topping on their Bigfoot.) The only respectable car in our fleet, Bill's shiny, sky blue Chevrolet Corsica, travels to Coeur d'Alene every day and is rarely seen by the common folk around our town. When Bill comes home from work, locals think we have out-of-town company arriving.

So far, both the Corsica and our old Buick have managed to escape the injuries that so often set North Idaho cars apart from other personal motor vehicles—scars from strategically planned rock peltings. These occur daily on our area's roadways. It's always fun to pick out North Idaho cars in big cities like Spokane. You don't need to look for the "Famous Potatoes" on the license plate; spot craters and cracks across the front windshield, and you've found a friend or neighbor.

When driving our van, we peer through a transparent maze of lines reminiscent of William Least Heat Moon's notion of "blue highways." Our slowly forming windshield "map" started about three years ago with a thin line in what could be considered Phoenix, Arizona. Proceeding east across New Mexico and Texas, the crack eventually developed a northern route before winding back across Oklahoma and Colorado. It took about six months. Then, on one of our trips to Coeur d'Alene, we passed a semi full of pigs on Highway 95. That encounter left us with more than a swine aroma. The truck had scored a direct hit, propelling a small rock that left a huge depression in the Central Washington portion of our windshield map. And those were just the beginnings. Now our Dodge window highways traverse the entire United States. If we actually could take a trip following our rock-pelt roads, we might be gone for weeks.

When the first blemish occurred, Bill and I vowed to take

the van in for repairs as soon as the mud season ended. As seasoned residents of the area, we soon saw the futility of spending lots of bucks just to have other flying rocks initiate new routes across our view. So we now drive around in our experienced, scarred van feeling a bit self-conscious, like a kid with too many zits.

Yet sometimes our van's blemished appearance is kind of nice, because otherwise it would look exactly like the other three thousand charcoal gray caravans Lee Iacocca sold in North Idaho alone. With our unique system of roadways across the windshield and "Sandpoint Says No to Drugs," "Good Paper-*Spokesman-Review*," "KZZU," "Sandpoint Is a Rainbow Community," and "Life's a Beach" stickers plastered across the backside, we have no problem spotting our rig in a crowded K-Mart lot.

Our fleet of four has become more practical as our kids have entered their teens. I once vowed that my kids would not have their own wheels until they graduated from high school. "After all, I teach at the high school and they could ride there with me," I reasoned. "I can take them wherever they need to go." That theory lasted about as long as my son Willie's first regular high school basketball season. Three months' worth of evenings spent taxiing back and forth between school and home changed my mind. I couldn't wait for Willie's sixteenth birthday and his night driver's license.

Willie drives the old Ford pickup, and so far he's been a good boy who's given me no reason to worry about his responsibility with a vehicle. My initial fears might just have stemmed from my own childhood driving exploits, which gave my folks numerous reasons to be a bit reluctant to turn a set of keys over to me. My desire to have pre-drivers' license relationships with a car came precociously early. My first real encounters took place in the front seat of a 1949 Ford sedan and on the metal perch of a 1954 Ford tractor. Both experiences developed my ability to

think on my feet and delegate authority, and one led to my first—
and last—attempt to run away from home.

*My illicit Ford sedan experience occurred on a sunny sum-
mer morning, when Mother decided to get me out of the house
and her hair by giving me the job of washing the car.* Backing it
out of its usual parking spot in the driveway, she pulled onto
the front lawn while I went inside the house and changed into
my swimsuit.

I had been at the job just a few minutes when Mother came
outside and announced that she needed to go to town. Since the
boys were off fishing at Sand Creek and Harold was working
his shift at the city water filtration plant, her departure in
Harold's pickup meant I would be home alone for at least thirty
minutes while she drove down to the Boyer Store for some milk,
bread, and Salem cigarettes.

Although I was just nine years old, I knew that "home alone"
demanded that you fly into forbidden action. My brothers had
taught me well. We were masters at committing every household crime with one eye on what we were doing and the other
focused down Boyer, watching for family vehicles to appear just
past Joe Carter's place about half a mile south of the house.
That first sighting meant we had precisely one minute to destroy incriminating evidence and get everything back in order
before the folks rolled into the driveway.

When the three of us were involved, one was always ap-
pointed to the watch—usually me. My age and sex generally
left me mere witness as the boys made forays into Mother and
Harold's closets, the freezer, or the bread drawer. On that particular morning, however, I had the place to myself. My only
challenge was to keep watch while committing the act. The object of my crime? It stood right in front of me, dripping with
water from the garden hose.

I started my assigned task, hose in one hand, towel in the other. It was important to put on a good show for Mother so that she would go to town confident that my chore would keep me busy and out of trouble long enough for her to do her errands. Once the dust cloud from the pickup had disappeared, though, I wasted no time dropping the hose and towel.

The car sat shining with water. I climbed in. After surveying the dashboard, ignition, and floor pedals, I practiced grabbing the steering wheel and driving down a make-believe highway, turning right, left, right, and slamming on the brakes, with sound effects along the way. An occasional honk kept stragglers out of my path.

The fantasy did not satisfy me.

"Why not try the real thing?" I reasoned. "She'll be gone for quite a while." I was a pushover for my own argument. The time seemed right for my first encounter with a real live automobile, and the key was in the ignition. (North Idaho residents in the 1950s rarely worried about car theft.) With one foot on the gas and the other on the brake, I turned the key.

The engine turned over, but the car jerked and died. I tried again, but the same thing happened. I jumped out of the car and looked down the road to see that Mother wasn't coming, then got back into position. Surveying the situation, I decided that pulling on the knob extending from the right side of the steering wheel might have something to do with getting the thing going. Once again I turned the key. The motor turned over and the car lurched a few feet backward with the same reaction as a heart attack victim undergoing defibrillation, and on the next try it did the same. At least I was getting it to move. My body pumped adrenaline.

My focus became twofold: jump out and check the road, jump back in and try again. I tried different approaches each time in an effort to figure out how to get the thing moving a little further. Having never really paid attention to all of Mother's driving techniques, I realized that I was going to have to watch her more closely in the future. I knew about the brake and the steering wheel and the horn, but the correct use of the gearshift and that other pedal on the left side of the floor had me in a quandary.

After several backward burps that had taken the car precisely two feet across the lawn, I hit on the right combination of foot and hand. On about my ninth attempt to get the rig rolling, it shot backward about one hundred feet—across the rest of the lawn, out the driveway, and onto the grassy patch next to the front pasture. Experiencing the sensation astronauts must feel immediately after launch, I remained paralyzed until the image of the fence around the pasture shot thought my mind.

"Oh, God! No!" I screamed, smashing the brake to the floor. My body lunged forward, leaving me in an embrace with the steering wheel. I'm sure a mild whiplash occurred, but my brain was too occupied with, "Whatcha going to do now?" to evaluate bodily damage.

"I've got to get this thing to go forward," I thought, hopping out and peering down the road in search of signs of Mother. Time was of the essence. Enough had happened in the previous ten seconds to make it seem as though an hour had passed and Mother's return was overdue.

"Where are Mike and Kevin when I need them?" I asked myself. "They'd get a good laugh out of this one. They'd heckle and blackmail me for months." I knew, in spite of their teasing, that we had an unwritten pact to help one another out of a fix, thus avoiding our mother's one-for-all, all-for-one punishment system. But I was in it alone this time; no boys were around.

I surveyed the situation in front of me. The good news was that the car had not yet run into the woven-wire fence surrounding the pasture, but instead had chosen a straight backward path that avoided the giant white pines and the snowberry bushes surrounding our front lawn. The bad news was that I had no idea how to get the car to go forward. First I tried to push it, but it rolled all of ten centimeters with each desperate effort. Abandoning this plan, I jumped back into the driver's seat and started the motor again. Since I still had no clue as to the purpose of the gearshift, I just repeated what I'd done before. Mother's car belched backward once more, moving enough for its rear tail light to become lodged within one of the openings in the fence. I jumped out again. I knew I was in deep trouble because the clock was ticking away with every bead of sweat that dripped profusely from my brow.

I looked off down the road once more—still no sign of Mother. While checking out the scene, though, I spotted a potential savior. In a hay field across the road, Mr. Clarence Best, our seventy-five-year-old neighbor, was bouncing around on his International tractor at approximately forty miles per hour, dragging his overworked and much misunderstood New Holland baler behind him. Mr. Best was known around our house for his inefficiency with tractors, mowers, balers, and any other farm equipment that rumbled over the fields of his dairy farm. That day was no exception. He sped around like a greyhound pursuing a rabbit, spewing approximately one lonely bale per round from the back chute of his baler and dribbling hundreds of flakes of loose timothy, leaving "Mr. Best trails" around the field. As usual, he traveled across the field so fast that looking backward to inspect his job could have turned fatal.

Disregarding my improper hay field apparel, I took off across Boyer and climbed through the barbed-wire fence. The fact that I was barefoot did not occur to me until I took my first step into the field of stubble and stickers. Any masochist will agree that a newly mown field of hay can rank right up there as a source of self torture. That morning, my need for self-preservation helped me to ignore the bloody holes in the bottoms of my feet; I knew that each anguished step across the razor-sharp stubble could not come anywhere near the humiliation and punishment Mother could dish out. Desperation is the mother of invention—I came up with a new dance, "stubble trouble," which involved intricate steps and the bodily contortions of a Canadian honker, to get Mr. Best's attention as he rumbled past.

I tried yelling at him from about thirty feet away when he made his first pass. No dice. The equipment roared on northward. I'd have to wait for the next go-round, which wouldn't be long, but every second counted. I took a few more painful steps forward while waiting for my next chance. This time I stood only two windrows (about twelve feet) away as Mr. Best rounded the southeast corner of his route. Surely he would spot me. Who could miss a frantic nine-year-old in a blue bathing suit waving wildly in the middle of a field?

Mr. Best could.

My desperate gestures failed to draw his attention and his tractor from the straight-and-narrow. With cupped hands, I yelled as loud as I could when he passed by again, but my only answer was a mouthful of chaff that came flying my way as his equipment roared past on its mission northward.

I knew that the next time I would have to make a real effort. I would stand in his pathway waving both my arms high in the air, jumping up and down, yelling and screaming. If that didn't work, it wouldn't matter anyway. I could see the baler swooping me up and chopping away at my body, its mangled parts packed and deposited as just another lump in Mr. Best's field. The hay hands would wonder what kind of feed Mr. Best was trying on his Holsteins that year as they grabbed a bale of Marianne and flung me on to the wagon. I knew even that lurid scenario might just be a better option than what was going to happen if Mr. Best didn't stop and help me get the car back before Mother came home.

Again Mr. Best rounded the corner and started in my direction. I began to jump and wave as he got closer but he still seemed oblivious or in some sort of hypnotic state. I danced some more. He kept on coming. I jumped really high and waved really wildly. No reaction. Then I began yelling really loudly. He was getting so close that I had to make some quick decisions. Which method of suicide seemed better—death by baler or mother? As I pondered my fate, Mr. Best suddenly slammed on the brakes, bringing his tractor and baler to rest just in the nick of time. I jumped back to the side and tried to look calm while he turned off the engine.

Mr. Best leaned on the steering wheel, dressed in his usual greasy outfit of jeans and blue work shirt with baseball cap. Covered with dust and chaff, he looked pretty grisly, but Mr. Best usually looked pretty grisly. He had lost his teeth. A beanpole about six feet tall, he had kind blue eyes, perpetually stubbly cheeks, and the most prominent Adam's apple I'd ever seen. He was no matinee idol, but he'd always been around to help in our early childhood years, giving us rides to town when we didn't have a car. He butchered our steers and helped any time we needed anything to do with farming. Past experience told me I could count on him once more.

Sweat trickled down his dirty face as he sat looking at me, no doubt curious about my sudden dramatic performance. "What's the problem?" he asked.

"I've got to ask you a favor," I began. "I was washing Mother's car over there in the front yard, and I accidentally backed it into the fence. Could you possibly go over and put it back where it belongs?"

Mr. Best looked over to our yard. "I'm kinda in a hurry to get this field done," he replied. "My crew's comin' to pick it up."

"It won't take long," I assured him. "Besides, you need to get it done before my mother comes back from town."

My nerve at that moment was a bit unusual for a child, but I'd always had a tendency to be outgoing with people, even strangers. However, even I had never been so assertive. Something within told me I had no time to beat around the bush or to allow Mr. Best any opportunity to say no.

"Okay," he said. "I'll go over there with ya." Leaving tractor and baler behind, he walked across the field. I did my best to keep up with him, although my feet felt like I'd been walking on prickly pears by that time. As he entered the driveway, Mr. Best (in typical male fashion) surveyed the wreckage and uttered several "Hmms" before finally deciding to enter the car.

I directed him to return Mother's Ford to the exact spot where it had been parked for its bath. He did so, got out, and started back toward the field. Thanking him profusely for his fine help, I made one more request of him before he could get out of the yard. "Could you please not tell my mother about this?" I pleaded. "She would be really unhappy to know that I've been driving the car."

He assured me that he would keep his mouth shut. I really liked Mr. Best. "What a friend," I thought, while watching him amble back to his work. It turned out to be my lucky day, because he was once again circling his hay field when Mother pulled into the driveway. I was off Scot-free.

Or so I thought. The telephone rang that afternoon right after Mother's favorite soap opera. Lying on my bed looking at cobwebs hanging from the ceiling, I tuned into Mother's conversation. At first it was the usual boring stuff, but then I started hearing some ominous words.

"She what? . . . What time was this? . . . Where was it parked? . . . He had to stop baling? . . . What else did she say?"

Mr. Best's approval rating took a big dip.

When the telephone conversation ended, Mother wasted no time coming to my room. "Where did you get the idea that you could drive the car?" she yelled. "Who do you think you are? You've got gall, bothering Mr. Best while he's working."

I had no ability to defend myself. I was skilled at finding creative projects but often lacked the know-how to talk myself out of the trouble that came with them. Slumped over on the edge of my bed with hands folded, I maintained a forlorn fixation on the floor as Mother made it clear that I would not be driving again until I was old and gray.

Old and gray came earlier than Mother had anticipated.
I was about twelve when she and Harold left for town one Saturday afternoon. Again, I was "home alone," since my brothers had gone on one of their mountain hikes from Sandpoint to Bonners Ferry. It was July again, too, haying season. I sat on the granary step, just inside the barnyard, as the family pickup headed out the driveway. That step was my favorite spot. I loved to spend hours there, especially on summer mornings when I could listen to meadowlarks and robins competing for the airwaves and watch the sun come up over Scotsman Peak in the Cabinet Mountains.

Although the step had its share of splinters waiting to ambush my rear end, it proved the best place for playing with kittens. Usually all I had to do was plop down and the latest batch would appear and race to claw their way up my bare leg and find a perch on my neck. I enjoyed talking to them as they purred and tickled me with their damp, miniature noses.

Playing with kittens was not always the easiest job in the world, because another sort of herd gathered at the granary as soon as its members eyed me heading there. Our horses were not dumb. They could be clear down in the pasture snipping off timothy or clover heads, but somehow their keen horse senses would alert them and one would announce to the group, "Marianne just sat down on the step. Let's get up there and bug her. Maybe she'll give us a treat."

Seldom did more than two or three minutes pass before I looked up to a forest of brown, white, or spotted noses, all wiggling and waiting for me to step inside and grab a handful of oats for them to fight over. If I didn't move, I could count on at least one set of velvety lips molesting my hair. They must have sensed that I didn't take a daily bath and there might be some goodies hidden within the snarls of my naturally curly but always messy mop-top. My daily summer routine became: sneak to the step, play with kittens, tolerate the noses for as long as possible, give up, get the grain, and get out of there.

On one particular July afternoon, the heat must have dulled my friends' senses, since no one, feline or equine, showed. I actually got bored enough to stick my head between my knees. Staring at the ground, I spotted a scrawny little twig and scratched out sketches in the dirt surrounding the step. After my folks left, this artistic challenge failed to inspire me, as did most things on hot summer afternoons. But soon, after I sat lumplike on the step and gazed around at the front pasture and the apple trees on the opposite side of the rail fence, my eyes zeroed in on a possible project near the big barnyard gate: Harold's gray Ford tractor.

Harold had left his beloved tractor parked parallel to the gate after mowing the front field that morning. With no horses or kittens to distract me, from my mind burst a fantastic plan. The moment was perfect—no brothers, no parents, no obligations, no impediments. The tractor sat there inviting me to just climb on and drive around the barnyard.

In the years since my first driving adventure I had observed Mother's technique behind the wheel of her new Ford Ranchwagon and had paid more attention to what she did with her feet. A little older, more mature, and more aware than I had been the last time I sat behind the wheel, I felt confident that I could pull off a successful driving experience.

Throwing my twig aside, I jumped up and walked over to the tractor, which had a mower hanging at an angle off its right side. I climbed on and sat down in the metal seat. Placing my feet on the pedals, I turned the key and pushed the starter button. The tractor fired up on the first try. Then I grabbed the metal rod extending to the right under the steering wheel. It took only a moment for me to learn that this device revved up the engine. The farther down I pulled it, the louder the tractor roared. At that time I had no concept o the connection this device had with the tractor's ability to go fast; it just sounded pretty impressive. After playing with this noise enhancer for a while, I decided to go on to bigger and better things.

I had learned enough to know that the gearshift sticking up below me had a lot to do with getting the tractor to move. I'd also watched Harold push down one of the pedals whenever he worked with the gearshift, so I did the same. When I first moved the black knob on top of the shift, the tractor died, to my disappointment. But by repeating my earlier procedure I got it started again. As I did this, rotating my head every thirty seconds or so to check for parents, my confidence grew. Things were going right.

Thoughts of how nice it would be to show Mother and Harold I could drive raced through my head. Maybe Harold would let me help in the hay field. I could see myself driving the Ford across the front field and pulling a wagon while my brothers merely hurled bales of hay at each other. Mine was a great future.

The future had to wait. I knew how to start the tractor and how to rev its motor, but I still had to get the thing to go. Cruel history soon repeated itself, since on the second try, the tractor moved—in the wrong direction. It must have gotten word from the '49 Ford, however, since it lurched backward toward the same pasture as that car had years earlier. My newfound knowledge and presence of mind enabled me to use the brake and stop the tractor before it hit the fence. The motor died at the same moment.

Discouraged, I mulled over the philosophical implications. Was the tractor sending me a message? Was I doomed to go only backward and never forward? In an effort to dispel that depressing thought, I determined that I would not give up until I had made some sort of forward motion.

"I'd better study this thing," I said to myself, anxiously glancing down the road. After looking at all the options, I reasoned that I had probably put the gearshift in the wrong position. Firing up the engine once more and pulling the throttle down for dramatic effect, I manipulated the shiny black shift knob to another setting. Letting up on one of the pedals, I held on to the steering wheel as the tractor lunged forward. Then I slammed on the brake, killing the motor just as the tines on the mowing sickle decided to attack the gate.

This situation was not good. A torrent of sweat descended my face as I peered desperately down Boyer. Still no folks. "This can't happen," I groaned. "Why do these things happen to me? Why do I always have all the bad luck?" Stewing was going to do no good. I needed to take quick offensive action.

Once more, I started the tractor, knowing I must put it in reverse to get it unstuck from the gate. I tried to move the gearshift. It would not budge. I pushed down on it with force. Nothing happened. Frantic, I grabbed the shift and tried to choke it with both hands, but it failed to respond to physical abuse. Then I reasoned that maybe it *had* moved and that I ought to try to get the tractor moving one more time. Letting up on the clutch, I again held onto the steering wheel. The tractor jerked forward. The sadistic sickle penetrated at least three inches into the wooden rails of the gate.

There was no way I could allow Mother and Harold to pull into the driveway and see this. There would be no way to explain, no brothers to blame. Further attempts to get the fiendish Ford to do what I wanted were not likely to work, and I was doomed if I didn't do something immediately. So I acted on my last option.

Jumping from the tractor, I scrambled over the fence and ran out the driveway. Spotting a red pickup coming down the road about three hundred feet from the driveway, I leaped into the middle of the road, and began flagging it down. As the truck rolled to a stop, I could see two men inside. The driver leaned out his window.

"I've got a problem, " I shrieked. "I was driving our tractor and got the mower caught in the fence and I need some help."

Inside the pickup two identical, generic men sat looking at me. Both wore round-brimmed hats. Neither showed any emotion—no surprise, no shock, no friendliness, no humor—as they listened to my plea. Neither responded. Both just looked at me with blank, robotic expressions.

"The tractor's just inside our barnyard," I said while motioning to the left.

Still facially unresponsive, they nevertheless turned into the driveway as I ran behind their truck. The two strangers parked and got out. They both wore green work jeans and green work shirts. They were the same size and shape. Their faces revealed no distinct personalities. If there had been experiments in cloning back then, my two Good Samaritans could have been the results. Whoever had concocted these two had forgotten to throw in a dash of personality.

They said nothing as they looked over the tractor situation, then went silently through another gate into the barnyard. One stood and looked while the other climbed on the tractor and started the engine. They both surveyed the situation further as I showed them the tracks the tractor had left before its recent trip across the barnyard.

"It needs to be right back here," I said, pointing to the ground near the gate. I felt better by the second. These men were saving my life. A few minutes and the tractor would be back where it belonged; they'd be on their way, and Mother and Harold would be spared the worry of which creative punishment they'd have to inflict on me for this latest crime.

My euphoria was short-lived. I had been concentrating so hard on showing them exactly where to park the tractor that I had failed to notice Harold's green Ford pickup coming down the road from town.

While the men continued their job, I trotted through the gate to meet my parents. As their pickup stopped, I calmly announced, "Oh, Mother and Harold, I was driving the tractor and got the mower caught in the fence. These nice men volunteered to come and put it back for me."

This spirit of bravado and matter-of-fact reporting did nothing to dull their rage as they watched a man they'd never laid eyes on drive Harold's personal farm tractor. In spite of their shock, Mother and Harold had the decency to play along with my performance. We all acted like the event was perfectly normal. We were all adults, or so I thought for the next few moments. Surely Mother and Harold would strike up a friendship with these guys. They'd all get to talking. Then I could slip off into the woods and disappear for a while if their parental rage hadn't fully subsided.

Such hopes didn't pan out. As soon as the first clone climbed off the tractor, Harold thanked them both. Nothing else was said. The silent strangers got in their pickup and drove off. For years after that day I kept my eye out for the two but never saw them again—proving once and for all that Boyer served as my highway from Heaven and that they were my guardian angels.

If Boyer led to Heaven, the barnyard pulled me back to my personal Hell. The lecture began as soon as the red pickup disappeared down the road. "Who do you think you are? Where did you get the nerve? You're going to be grounded for life!" Mother promised. Harold just stood there looking disgusted, clearly wounded by the knowledge that within the space of half an hour three people—two total strangers—had invaded his space and laid hands on his private farm implement.

The scene was too much for me. "I'm leaving home," I yelled, taking off at a dead run out the barnyard gate and through the yard. Leaving home could be the only escape from years of bedroom confinement, dirty looks, and my family's overall disgust with my misdeed. "I'll start a new life," I reasoned, cutting across the front yard and slipping through the bushes near the garage.

"I'll call the sheriff!" Mother barked from the barnyard.

My life once more went into reverse, just like the two vehicles. Head hanging, I stayed home to accept my punishment.

I did not drive again until my senior year at Sandpoint High School, when I took driver's training, during which we learned how to drive a car with an automatic transmission. This I knew was a plot between my parents and the school system, since every vehicle on the Tibbs place had a standard transmission. I received a driver's license when I was eighteen, but it did me no good until the following year when Mother left town for a couple of weeks. That Catch-22 held because no one in my family wanted to teach me to drive with a clutch.

They hadn't counted on my friend Peggy Glazier. She came to visit one day while Mother was in New York for Mike's graduation at West Point and Harold was at work. As Peggy and I sat around the kitchen table enjoying a cup of coffee, the subject of driving came up. She couldn't believe that I was unable to drive any of the family vehicles. Peggy is now a real estate agent. She must have been developing her sales technique even then, because she convinced me that she could have me driving a stick shift within an hour. We climbed inside Mother's car and Peggy's prediction came true. I drove the Ranchwagon all around the neighborhood with no problems. Peggy left. A day or so later, I told my folks about my success behind the wheel. Surprisingly, they allowed me to touch the car and even drive it.

Since then, except for one fender-bender and a few speeding tickets, I've managed to improve if not erase my earlier reputation and generally keep my vehicles moving in the direction they're supposed to go. And if I ever need help, I know how to coerce any reluctant Samaritan who happens by.

Sunday Gambles

I had mixed feelings in July 1989 when Governor Cecil Andrus started the lottery in Idaho.

As a result of the passage of a controversial measure, "Try Your Luck" and "Fill Your Pocket Fantasy" tickets suddenly started appearing in supermarkets and convenience stores throughout the Gem State.

I voted for the lottery. Or did I? The preceding November I had voted "yes" for something, and thought it was the lottery. Then one of my friends told me he had voted "no" so we'd have a lottery. Another said she had voted "yes" so we wouldn't have any form of gambling in Idaho. Apparently, more people thought "no" meant "yes" and voted "no" than thought "yes" meant "no" and voted "yes." I'm still scratching my head about the strategy, but the measure passed. I guess it's the new politics of the twentieth century.

Anyway, I got what I wanted, so why was I so ambivalent? My wavering had nothing to do with the evils of gambling. I believe in gambling. I love to put my two dollars on the horses at Playfair in Spokane, and my name is always on Coach Ron the Greek's betting board at Sandpoint High School for the Super Bowl or World Series. If I voted wrong on the lottery question, it was out of ignorance, not indignation.

My annoyance with Idaho gambling stemmed from the availability of lottery tickets. No longer would our family need to take Sunday drives to Newport, Washington, for the dual purposes of dumping the trash and visiting the Safeway store for jelly doughnuts and Washington lottery scratch tickets. Cruising over to Washington to buy lottery tickets had helped my husband Bill and children Willie and Annie keep one of the most sacred and memorable traditions of my childhood years—the Sunday drive.

The gray days of January, February, and March cause many North Idaho families to act like a herd of hysterical horses milling around the close quarters of the barnyard. They need a break. A change of scenery. A moment or two of fantasy. For the Love family, the twenty-five-mile journey to Newport along Highway 2—overlooking the deep blue waters of the Pend Oreille River, passing through Dover, Wrenco, Laclede, and Priest River, finally crossing the Idaho/Washington border—satisfied our need for wintertime variety.

Before each shopping spree, I frisked every pocket in every piece of clothing I owned, then rummaged through the candy wrappers, paper clips, grocery receipts, and pen caps at the bottom of my purse in an exhaustive search for any stray nickel, dime, or quarter that hadn't found its way to a vending machine that week. At Safeway, Bill and the kids made a beeline for the bakery as I totaled my pile of change to determine just how many scratch tickets I could buy that week. At a dollar a ticket, usually two or three chances for wealth were possible. After all transactions were completed, we regrouped at the car for the suspense-filled moments of scratching each ticket, ever so slowly. The ultimate reward was a walk back to the store to claim free tickets—which invariably turned out to be losers. On other occasions, when we felt particularly wealthy, we'd go a block down the street to the Newport Quik Stop to play the numbers game for the Lotto drawing.

Gambling was certainly not the sole purpose of these after-church excursions. Of course not. The real reason for our afternoon jaunts was to continue the wonderful tradition initiated by my parents in the 1950s. Mother and Harold viewed Sunday drives as great opportunities to promote togetherness and to introduce us to the deer, trees, and mountain roads of the Idaho Panhandle and western Montana. We kids didn't always concur. When I reflect on some of the places my dad took us, I deduce the true origin of my present affinity for games of chance.

During my childhood, Tibbs family drives occurred in the dreary winter months, a period featuring the weather phenomenon some of us cynically call "North Idaho Gray." The outings became more frequent during March and April, however, when Harold renewed his annual resolve to return, lock, stock, and barrel, to his beloved Montana where the big sky was blue, the buffalo roamed, and there was no such barnyard abomination as foot-deep mud. He resented slogging through our Idaho slop, especially during calving season.

However, since Harold knew deep in his heart that we'd never permanently leave the farm we had built, he compromised. Our trips to Montana were temporary; he headed the family there for Sunday outings as soon as Mass ended. On a typical Sunday, we left church, changed our clothes, and, with some trepidation, prepared for an afternoon of family fun. For my two brothers and me, this involved acts of procrastination performed in our respective bedrooms.

Our folks sat impatiently in their 1958 Ford, a four-door Ranchwagon, armed with a box of Bacon Thins and the binoculars, impatiently honking the horn in an effort to get the three of us to hurry. In the house, I slowly combed my hair (which I seldom did any other time), straightened my collar, picked up a week's worth of dirty socks, and otherwise kept occupied, all the while listening for my brothers' departure from the house. When the incessant honking warned me that I'd better get a move on, I leisurely strolled out the door, confident that I had outlasted Mike and Kevin. My staying power meant I could sit next to the window in relative comfort instead of being folded up in my usual position straddling the hump.

But, usually, there they stood, one by each door, resplendent in untucked, plaid flannel shirts, baggy trousers, and ugly black oxfords, posing as perfect gentlemen. They held the doors open for me, their helpless little sister. In a less-than-ladylike fashion, I stomped past these pseudo-gents, finding my way to the dreaded middle position of the back seat, once again the underdog in the eternal two-against-one struggle. The boys smirked triumphantly as the car was backed out of the driveway and directed east down Highway 200 toward the Big Sky country, Harold's Montana homeland, his Valhalla with white-faced cattle and no mud.

These trips, poignant for Harold, were learning experiences for me. When I wasn't being poked, punched, or pinched—usually by Kevin—I observed with meager solace that my knees were just barely missing my chin. I looked out the window. I learned something else, too—the drives aroused my awareness of just how minimal was the capacity of my bladder.

Harold, like others of his gender, refused to stop at rest rooms, although gas stations in Kootenai, Trestle Creek, Hope, and Clark Fork had them. Consequently, my total concentration eventually focused on my internal water balloon. Mile after mile, pothole after pothole, I felt my bladder inflate to what was certainly the size of a beach ball. Every time the car succumbed to a surprise pothole attack, the urgency of my need to relieve myself made me even more uncomfortable. I actually became oblivious to brothers and their rude behavior. I sat paralyzed, staring straight ahead, feverishly tapping on my knee, all thoughts focused on my bouncing bladder as I conjured up the nerve to beg for a pot stop.

"Could you p-l-e-a-s-e stop up there by a tree so I can go to the bathroom?" I blurted out at last.

Harold begrudgingly rolled to a stop, interrupting his push to rack up as many Montana miles as possible, and allowed me a break from my misery. Even that was a Pyrrhic victory. Squatting behind a spruce in the tall and ticklish wet grass and enduring dank winter air on my bottom side made me wonder why I had ever left the car, but the total relief and the thought of relative comfort for another fifteen minutes gave me the spirit to return to the forthcoming sarcastic jeers from my brothers.

Our drives were also mathematical adventures, since "Count the Deer" ranked highest among the methods designed to minimize back-seat brawls. My brother Kevin's proud position in Montana's fraternity of "Great White Hunters" can be traced directly to these calculating competitions. He always spotted the most moth-eaten mulies and shaggy whitetails. To this day, I still question whether all those brush piles he counted were indeed deer, but Kevin said they were, so I didn't risk the pain that challenging his word might produce.

Although somebody always seemed to know our final destination, we kids were not always sure just where we were going and why. The lure of adventure often led Harold up some obscure mountain road, and the true test of just how well the Ford was built presented itself as we scraped bottom for several miles. All fighting in the back seat was put on hold while everyone but the driver said fervent "Hail Marys" in the hope that we wouldn't become high-centered in some wilderness spot unknown to any other humans and inhabited only by man-hungry bears.

Two excursions into the backcountry stand out in my mind. The first led us southeast of Clark Fork one April day when Mother happened to be nine months pregnant with my little sister Laurie. Harold chose this experience to let us know first-hand that he really had been inspired by Robert Frost's poem, "The Road Not Taken." The road that no one else had *ever* taken led our family up the mountain, all right, but when we learned we were driving through the Bonneville power-line system, Mother almost went into labor. During the second escapade, Harold's roundabout route took us through an unknown and unappreciative farmer's barnyard near Hot Springs, Montana.

One might question the sentimental value of these adventures, especially since I seemed to be miserable much of the time we drove up and down those country roads. Sure, there were uncomfortable and occasionally unnerving moments. But the images of eagles perching in white pine trees along the Clark Fork River near Noxon, rainbow trout and big ugly suckers co-existing in the crystal clear, still waters at the Johnson Creek bridge south of Clark Fork, and a brown bear bounding up a hillside near Hope shine brighter than my memories of physical discomfort.

These days the hope of striking it lucky with a winning lotto ticket has provided a new incentive for my own nuclear family to head out occasionally on Sunday afternoons. We haven't found our bonanza with the scratch of a ticket, but the magnificent sights of our weekend drives remind us that our true wealth lies all around us in God's Country. It's a great pleasure to know that there are enough excursions out there for—yes—a month of Sundays.

Great Horned Cows

Mother married Harold for numerous reasons. She didn't have a husband. She liked him. He had a Ford tractor.

Harold married Mother for similar reasons. He liked her. He had no wife, no kids, and no land for his Hereford cattle. I'm not so sure Harold was looking for kids, but we three Brown kids came with Mother's forty acres of land and her love. It worked out, and virtually every aspect of their union eventually ended up interdependent.

For forty years, Mother and Harold have built their relationship on love, work, and daily challenges created by the advantages (or disadvantages) of their marital agreement. The tractor, a predecessor to numerous others over the years, tilled

the land. The land fed the cattle. And the cattle shaped the kids; that herd of horned Herefords maimed our bodies, stifled our self-esteem, and tested our tolerance in astonishing degrees.

Cows did for our lifestyle what psychological tests do for rats. Our relationships with the bovine critters roaming our fields elicited reactions that could provide a semester's work for a psychotherapy student. Gloria Steinem tells talk show addicts to examine their early childhood relationships to understand why they act and feel the way they do, and I have. I'm convinced that sharing these tales of Milford (the flat-backed herd bull), his daughter Millie (queen bee of Bonner County cattle shows), Dorothy (hater of hypercritical cattle judges), Billy (the ornery cuss who tacked me to the box stall wall), and Mary Elephant (the homely but protective matriarch of the barnyard) will provide plenty of insight to my adult behavior patterns.

As a new father of three preteens, Harold got us started doing cow chores early on. Later, when we were old enough, we could join the Mountain View Livestock 4-H Club, which he happened to be leading at the time. Harold held the strong belief that kids who worked with animals were taught many lessons about life. His faith proved true. We learned self-discipline, responsibility, and initiative during the spring and summer days spent preparing our individual projects for the Bonner County Fair. As a bonus, Mike and Kevin got a taste of high finance when they fattened up steers as projects.

I soon learned that I didn't want to take a fat steer to market. Mother and I broke down in uncontrollable sobs at the Saturday night stock sales while innocent, loyal friends like Kevin's steer Festus faithfully followed their owners one last time around the indoor arena, and twangy auctioneer voices barked out their price-per-pound death sentences. The emotional price was too high for us. We stayed away from the show barn after the auctions, waiting until Sunday morning to go get our brushes and tack box, since seeing an empty rope halter tied to a manger could set us off once more.

I had joined 4-H when I was ten, but the first year was a bust. Mother thought I ought to limit myself to a few home economics projects in Lucille Hudon's Mountain View ABCs, the female adjunct to the livestock club. Cooking and arts and crafts projects were okay, but I just didn't think they did for the inside of me what the outside of a four-legged critter could. I longed to emulate my big brothers and have my very own live, breathing project.

I did get to learn about cows in Mrs. Hudon's club, but they were "purple cows" that came from a recipe in our 4-H cooking manual. You beat up grape juice and milk with the Sunbeam mixer. You drank the resulting concoction while sampling your wienie boat, a combination of hot dogs, melted cheese, and catsup meant to look like a sailboat. Then you were supposed to write about them in your University of Idaho Cooperative Extension record book. That's where I fell short.

When fair time rolled around and Mrs. Hudon asked for my record book, she "had a cow" of her own. "You haven't finished this book," she said. "All you've done is fill out the front cover."

I grunted.

"Where is the information that goes on the last three pages?" she continued. "What about your story? Did you write one?"

"I didn't know I was supposed to," I uttered.

Mrs. Hudon wasn't impressed. At fair time she had more to do than sit down and fill out the missing information from six months of cooking and arts and crafts projects. Thus, one of the guiltiest episodes of my young life was revealed.

I was a failure.

The message came out loud and clear as Mother mercilessly assessed my oversight. I remember the scene as if it were yesterday. "You'll never amount to anything," she announced after talking to my leader and finding out just why I would not be able to take my cookies and pine baskets to the fair. As she stood at the barnyard gate that September afternoon, I stood a few feet away, ready to escape. "You didn't do your record book. You were supposed to write down all the times you baked cookies and made that lumpy vanilla pudding," she fumed. "Why didn't you?" In truth, Mother had not been aware of the record book requirement either; nevertheless, her wrath made up for the oversight. That scolding still reverberates every time I'm tempted to half-do any job.

I remember the low, scummy feeling that hung around for months afterward. I had not completed the requirements for my first year of 4-H. No ribbons, no premium money, no recognition at achievement night. I felt the sting and resolved that such dereliction of duty would not be repeated. It never has. The next year I resolutely doubled-up by retaking the first year projects along with a second year of cooking, sewing, and arts and crafts. I also landed my first spot on the roster of the Mountain View Livestock Club by virtue of my beef project, a lovely Hereford heifer named Dorothy, in honor of my mother's college roommate.

Dorothy—the heifer, that is—provided the much needed carrot to encourage my continued interest for home ec 4-H. If I cooked, sewed, and filled out my record book regularly, everyone would be happy. I could continue caring for my animal. Mrs. Hudon could see success as a leader. Mother could avoid embarrassment. I could join the ranks of my older brothers and get a cow ready for the fair.

Dorothy was a yearling heifer when Mother and Harold selected her as the best prospect in the herd for an eleven-year-old novice. She and I got along well that spring and summer as I brushed and combed her daily. She loved baths on hot July afternoons, and she cooperated as I attempted to master the coordination of walking around the barnyard, leading her, and carrying a show stick in my left hand.

That combination may sound easy, and it is for most people. But unlike most people, I missed out on the gene that promotes coordination of the lower extremities. As an infant, I was lucky I learned to walk. Since that time I have attempted other choreographed activities, including a college folk dancing class during which my instructor waylaid me one day after class, waited until all the other students had left, and asked, "Are you really trying?" The only thing that got me through that class was the written final. More recently, I foolishly showed up at an after-school session in line dancing. After attempting to master the "Achy Breaky Heart," mine was once more shattered after a mere five minutes of stumbling and tripping among the masses to whom God had given coordination and grace.

Needless to say, learning to walk around the barnyard keeping track of my cow with one hand and clutching my show stick with the other presented a formidable challenge. After a summer's work, however, I mastered the skill well enough to earn a blue ribbon in fitting and showing. I'm sure my strong suit was Dorothy's cleanliness. The judge could not detect a loose hair or fleck of dandruff as he rubbed his hand over her back. Hours of sanding away at her horns had paid off. Those horns glistened. Dorothy dazzled the crowd, behaving like a queen as we circled the arena, stopped, set up, and started again. She stood quietly each time the judge returned for inspection. My labors were rewarded.

When the class ended, Tommy Anselmo, Delbert Wood, and I stood proudly at the head of the pack of first-year beef members to receive our prizes, the only three blue ribbons awarded. I scanned the audience for family members. My parents were proud. I was proud. This 4-H business had turned around. I even did all right with my home ec projects; all my record books passed inspection. I succeeded. My 4-H future was bright—or so I thought. Dorothy had done so well for me that there was no need to discuss next year's beef project. We two were a team.

But Dorothy's attitude changed. The next year, she decided that behaving in the show ring was not her cup of tea. All 4-H beef members must show their animals in quality and fitting and showing, and quality came first. When Dorothy walked into the ring for her yearly inspection, the judge was not impressed. As a two-year-old, my project lacked some of the desired characteristics the judge was seeking. "Too bony. Not enough flesh," he decided, putting her in the red ribbon row.

Apparently Dorothy disagreed with his decision. As the judge, a livestock specialist from the University of Idaho, stood behind the microphone, justifying his placement, she started in on him. Suddenly I was standing with show stick in one hand and no heifer in the other. With her nose to the ground and her tail in the air, Dorothy made a beeline for her detractor, swooping past him with just inches to spare. The judge was in midsentence, still moving his lips, when his commentary was replaced by the bellowing of my heifer. Galloping past, Dorothy had caught his microphone, stand and all, with her horn. As she dragged it with her around the arena, the cord had to oblige and come along for the ride. So did the judge, since the cord was wrapped around his legs. He apparently had more coordination than I did, or had practiced a little line dancing, because he quickly escaped, avoiding permanent bodily injury.

The episode was a disaster for me, since it started the tongue-waggling about "that Brown girl" and "those darned horns." One of my ostensibly friendly critics, Bob Nesbitt, led the Sagle Yodeling Coyotes Livestock Club, whose membership had been brainwashed into believing that any animal with horns was related to the devil. From that day on, Bob ran an annual propaganda campaign aimed at me, hoping I would see the light about horned Herefords.

"When ya gonna saw them horns off that ol' critter?" he'd ask almost every time he'd see me. "Don'tcha know you could have a lot easier time if ya didn't have to deal with them?"

"Nope, not going to," I'd stubbornly reply.

Bob rattled off the litany of sensible reasons why I and all Bonner County fairgoers would be better off if I'd just get rid of Dorothy's horns. Although I still liked Bob in spite of this yearly harassment, the Tibbses were a horned Hereford family, and we'd stay that way. It didn't matter how many abrasions I collected when Dorothy's razor-sharp headdress accidentally scraped a pattern down my arm. Nor did it matter how many of those hot August hours I spent grinding and grubbing away at ridges and dirty cracks on Dorothy's horns in preparation for fitting and showing. I was proud to be leading a horned Hereford because those cattle were bigger, better, and classier than the polled (non-horned) whitefaces. At least that's what we Tibbses thought at the time.

Because of my disastrous show ring experience with Dorothy, Harold and Mother decided that as a third-year beef member I would graduate to Millie, the fifteen-hundred-pound daughter of Milford, Harold's newest bull. One wintry Sunday a few years previous, the entire family had gone down to Colfax, Washington, to visit the Frank Feenan ranch and select the right mate for Harold's cows. After a few hours of checking out the Feenan bulls, Harold selected FF Milliron 11, a yearling, to father our cows' calves. The Milliron strain was guaranteed free of dwarfism, which had infiltrated cattle bloodlines throughout the country. Although such critters were cute, they didn't bring smiles to the lips of cattlemen trying to make a living from the price per pound of their livestock. We had a couple of dwarf calves born on our place, so the herd needed new blood.

Milford, as we named him, was a handsome bull, definitely a Type B personality. As he grew into a fine-looking herd bull, his back became perfectly level—about three feet across if you stood at his side and tried to reach over it. Milford's back was so flat that one day he lay down in the pasture and started to roll over. Midway through the rotation, he was flat on his back with all four legs reaching for the sky, unable to roll either way. Someone discovered his predicament and went out to the field, grabbed his legs, and pulled him to one side, but the trauma probably taught Milford not to attempt such exercises in the future because we never had to rescue him again.

Our animals had to have patience to survive heckling and more from us kids. We believed anything that had four legs and weighed more than five hundred pounds ought to be broke to ride. Not all our cattle and horses agreed with us, and we've got the scars to prove it, but Milford was different. He loved personal attention. His anatomy posed a problem for conventional-style riding, however, since it was next to impossible to wrap one's legs around his big bull's barrel. Imagine doing the same with a kitchen table, and you'll grasp the situation.

But Kevin, who usually took the lead when it came to breaking cows, was inventive, and yearned to ride Milford, who was so cooperative and willing to please. So one day he had a brainstorm. Instead of sitting on the bull, Kevin would *stand* on his back and go for a ride. After putting the rope halter on, Mike and I stood at his head with the lead in hand while Kevin climbed aboard. Milford didn't seem to mind. Kevin got the mild-mannered bull into gear. He had no problem keeping his balance because Milford's back was so flat, and off they went, like circus performers, trotting through the woods. The scene was repeated whenever Mother and Harold happened not to be around to critique it.

The first time our parents saw their six-foot, four-inch son mounted on the noble Milford was the day the Joneses from Eltopia, Washington, came to call.

Showing animals off to company was a common form of entertainment around our house. Folks would show up and sit in the living room for about ten minutes of talking. Then either Mother or Harold would suggest, "Let's go out and look at the horses and cows." Everybody would get up and head out the door—everybody, that is, except we kids, who knew exactly where Mother hid the treats for the company. After a side trip to the cookie jar, we rejoined the yakkity-yakkers midway around the barnyard. While each horse and cow underwent a thorough inspection, accompanied by several historical anecdotes about how the critter had improved since arriving at the Tibbs ranch, we kids planned something to really wow the crowd.

Kevin performed his all-time spectacle for the Joneses. Mother, father, and their six kids had apparently never seen trees on their farm in the Palouse wheat fields. The kids wasted no time climbing ours, and soon were climbing everything on the place, including fences, light poles, and pines. The adults, visitors and residents, talked horses.

Meanwhile, Kevin disappeared.

His return was probably discussed for years afterward in our guests' farmhouse. Like a comic-book sighting of Superman, it stopped all conversation. Heads turned. Mr. Jones gasped, "What the heck is that?" His open mouth revealed an absence of teeth, suggesting he had dropped his dentures when he spotted Kevin out of the corner of his eye. Mr. Jones had plenty of corroborating witnesses that day to attest that he really had seen a huge young man standing on top of a great big Hereford bull that obediently trotted through our field. Mother and Harold normally would have been embarrassed, but having Eltopia kids climbing around the barnyard perimeters like monkeys in the jungle broke the sense of normality and hinted that anything was possible at the Tibbs ranch.

A chuckle here and a giggle there finally cut the silence. "Yup, this is our herd bull, Milford," Harold explained. "We got him down in your country." As Kevin dismounted, Harold calmly continued discussing the whys and wherefores of Milford. "He's been a good outcross for my herd," he told the still open-mouthed visitors. "We're getting some nice big replacement cows, and the calves are always a decent size for those first-calf heifers."

A few minutes later, after the rest of the tour and some more farm talk, the Eltopians gathered up their half-dozen climbing rug rats and drove off for an afternoon of square dancing. We never saw them again, and I still haven't figured out when Mr. Jones actually lost his dentures. We found no sign of them in the barnyard.

In addition to his suitability for barnyard circus acts, Milford proved to be a good herd bull. He sired some nice young cows, one of which was Millie. Millie was not only a pretty heifer from the start, but also showed leadership skills early on. It was easy to see that Milford's daughter had a future as a good calf producer, so I was thrilled when Mother announced at dinner one evening that she would be my 4-H project. "She should do well in quality, and she has such a nice disposition," Mother said. This was great news. I had become a successful junior cattle judge during my two previous years in 4-H, so I knew I had a cow to wow even the most outspoken horned Hereford critics. Bob Nesbitt would eat his words come September when he saw this beautiful animal amble down the fairgrounds loading ramp.

Millie did turn lots of eyes when she arrived at the Bonner County Fair that year. We took top blue in the quality category, and I came home with a high blue in fitting and showing. My reputation was changing and the naysayers, including Bob Nesbitt, remained somewhat quiet. The Dorothy stories had pretty much subsided.

The next year Millie produced her first in a long line of bull calves, Gilbert. My project could then include cow-calf, which meant an opportunity to win the cow-calf trophy sponsored by the Bonner County Cow Belles. My mother was a Cow Belle, and so were her friends. These ladies liked to keep track of the kid who won their trophy and always showed up in force when the 4-H beef show began. Each year for three years Millie and her calf won their award. Each year the ladies watched from the stands with expressions of great approval. This was all well and good, but there was an aspect of my cow-calf project that made me dread the sight of these polite, upstanding members of the community every year.

The first year I took Millie and Gilbert to the fair I learned some things about the protective instinct of mother cows and about the Cow Belles' disgusting sense of humor. As a solo act, Millie had always performed beautifully. In fact, she was such a shining example of what a cow should do when circling the show ring for inspection that we always let the younger 4-Hers practice with her before the fair. Millie was one of those rare cows that had the patience and instinct to know exactly how to act when little ten-year-olds took hold of the lead rope and show stick for the first time. Almost dwarfing the little kid beside her, she walked quietly, patiently, and carefully. She knew when to stop, where to put her feet, how to hold her head up, and exactly how to pose however long it took to properly show off for the practice judge in the barnyard show ring. She was a gem of a cow, or so I believed.

The gem was revealed to be fool's gold when Millie, now mother of Gilbert, entered the real show ring for my fitting and showing class. That year the 4-H beef show had moved to the outdoor arena, just a few feet from the Pend Oreille River, where one of McNall's shorthorns had decided to take an unauthorized swim during a livestock event a few years earlier. The McNalls and all others who tried to retrieve the errant critter were not happy about the animal's propensity for a new water sport. Everyone who witnessed that event knew the potential for cows out of control.

I wasn't worried, though, because I had Millie, and she was my pal. I had nurtured our relationship during hours of scratching and combing her beneath cottonwood trees on lazy summer afternoons. I trusted my cow implicitly. As we walked side by side into the ring, I was confident we would leave the ring with another blue ribbon and maybe a chance to compete for champion showman.

It didn't happen. The ring was about two hundred yards from the barn where Gilbert was tied to the manger and, as we entered, Millie suddenly decided she had strayed too far from her son's side. That moment I learned where her true loyalty lay—not with me. As we began to circle the arena, Millie's pace quickened. I tried to walk fast, rationalizing that maybe it would look good to the judge. But Millie continued to speed past Louise Bandy's Angus steer and Delbert Wood's Hereford and Jim McNall's shorthorn, and . . . .

As we rounded the turn in front of the Cow Belles' bleacher, I could see the ladies eyeing me, more than likely proud because we were this year's cow-calf winner. The first time we stopped and set up our animals, Millie stood still, all right, but she also decided it was a good time to call out for Gilbert.

"Moooooo-ooooooo! Moooooooo-ooooooooo!"

"Shut up!" I whispered, remembering what past livestock judges had thought of bellowing cows.

" M M M M M O O O O O O O - O O O O O O O O ! MMMMMMMOOOOOOO! MOO!" she continued while pulling her head away from my grip

I secured my hold on the lead.

Millie continued to bellow and started to circle around me,

pulling harder at the lead. I held on with all my might, willing myself to stay calm. The judge motioned for us to resume leading our animals around the ring, and I tried to comply. But Millie had assumed control. She had seen the judge's signal and had decided to take matters into her own hands—er, hooves. With steady, deliberate pressure, *she* began leading *me* around the ring, all the time bawling and begging for Gilbert to join her.

We passed in front of the Cow Belles again, and I could hear giggles and see amusement written all over their faces as Millie and I sped by. The judge motioned for us to stop and set up again. With all my energy, I jerked the chain on the show halter and brought the fifteen-hundred-pound maternal monster to a sliding stop. I wheeled around, quickly exchanging the show stick and the lead. I set Millie up on all fours and tried frantically to calm her down by scratching her belly.

It did the trick—for about ten seconds.

Then Millie regained control. The bellowing, the dragging, the racing around the ring escalated, as did the Cow Belles' insidious laughter. This was a bovine nightmare. If I had possessed the ability to pinch myself, I still would have awakened to the reality that my prized cow was making a total fool of me. But I held on while Millie continued to monopolize the attention of the judge, the other contestants, and those sadistic Cow Belles. I don't know which sound rang worse in my ears—the giggles or Millie's bellows. My misery all ran together.

The class seemed endless, especially after a show ring official intercepted me and asked if I could kindly tie my cow to the railing until the judging was completed. (This person was undoubtedly someone who had participated in the McNall river round-up.) Once Millie was secured to the fence, I finally let go of the lead. I had gripped it so tightly that my fingers remained curled as if suffering some grotesque deformity. While speeding around the ring, I had concentrated so much on trying to control Millie that pain was secondary, but on release my right hand burned as its veins began to function again.

My hand was not the only part of my anatomy that was burning. My Irish heritage began to show as Millie continued calling out for Gilbert and the Cow Belles tried (halfheartedly) to restrain their glee. Boiling within, I was humiliated as well, my summer's work destroyed. This ignominy was confirmed when the ring official walked over to where my cow and I stood and pulled a white ribbon from the shoe box and handed it to me. Bottom white.

"Thank you," I muttered begrudgingly, remembering the many lectures about sportsmanship from my mother.

"It's just as important to be a good loser as it is to be a winner," Mother had repeated at 4-H meetings. Of course, that platitude was meant for other kids, not us. My mother expected results, never anticipating that any of her children would ever lose, graciously or otherwise. Little did she or I know that my show ring tragedy would recur year after year.

Immediately after the Millie and Gilbert debacle, I vowed never to take her in fitting and showing again, as long as she had a calf. I resolved to train only calves and show Millie in the cow-calf competition where she could stand alongside them, leaving her maternal instincts and her voice at rest.

But fate dealt a sadistic hand.

The next year Millie had another bull calf, Sullivan. I worked all summer bathing, combing, leading, and showing him. He worked for me like a dream, and it appeared that I would not be embarrassed that year. We took the animals to the fair, and I reported to the beef superintendent to register for my classes. When it came to fitting and showing, I told the official I'd be showing my bull calf.

"No, you can't do that," she announced. "We can't allow 4-H members to show bulls in fitting and showing. Someone might get hurt."

"But he's only four months old," I argued.

"Sorry, that's the rule," she repeated with bureaucratic assuredness. "We cannot allow bulls in fitting and showing."

I couldn't believe my ears. I started asking around about the rule, but, sure enough, the livestock committee had decided it would be risky to allow members to show bulls in fitting and showing. Red tape assured me of another white ribbon. I still think it was a plot hatched by the Cow Belles to back me into a corner. I think they enjoyed my sideshow with Millie so much they infiltrated the ranks of the livestock honchos and said, "Let's make a rule so Marianne will have to show that crazy cow again. Wasn't it hilarious last year?" I'm sure this is what happened, because no matter how much I protested, no one showed me any empathy—least of all Bob Nesbitt. As I think of it, I'll bet he was in on it, too. It was his clandestine way of tricking me into admitting that horned Herefords really were for the birds, behaviorally speaking.

For the next two years, Millie and her bull calves won the Bonner County Cow Belles trophy for the best cow-calf combination at the fair. And each year, in exchange, the Cow Belles satisfied their fiendish senses of humor by watching my fitting and showing disintegrate from initial brilliance into a galloping race. The finish line was always that familiar spot along the railing. The reward was always the same, that familiar, ugly white ribbon—and one whole dollar, the fair premium for a summer's worth of work. Not exactly cost-effective. The Cow Belles were happy; the other 4-Hers, who were guaranteed that someone would be worse than they, were thrilled; and Bob Nesbitt probably grinned to himself for months afterward.

My 4-H career ended with my last year of high school, though my interest in cattle did not. During the summers between my years at the University of Idaho I selected the best prospects from Harold's herd to show at the Bonner County Fair's open class beef competition. By the time I figured out all the best combinations for competition, my string of show stock usually averaged eight to ten head. Taming calves that had never felt a human hand in their first three months of life, scrubbing several miles of dirty hides at a time, and just plain hauling the critters to the fairgrounds were logistical nightmares, especially when all these activities had to be kept secret from Harold.

Harold was no fan of the annual fair frenzy. "There's no need to go to all that work," he'd grumble. "We're not takin' any cows to the fair and that's final." For some reason he always hated to see people get involved in too much work, so he put a damper on our annual plans to show off the year's livestock crop. We never took him seriously, though; much behind-the-scenes activity took place. While he monitored the water flow at the filter plant, Mother and I schemed as to how we'd get those animals down there without his knowing. Somehow our strategy always worked, and somehow he always came around once he learned that Millie had again won grand champion cow. Harold then showed up at the beef barn, beaming from ear to ear, genuinely pleased that we had ignored his advice.

Cow shows were always a lot of work, heightened by good-natured competition. Every August, Denny Shields, who raised polled Herefords, came around to inspect our herd. The visit was Denny's way of scouting out the competition. Every summer he returned to map out his strategy for coming out ahead in the awards. I never really minded Denny's topping us because our friendship was what mattered—as did that pilgrimage to the church food booth for lunch with him afterward. Denny always sprung for the meal, no matter the outcome of the show.

Open class competition gave Millie a chance to erase the earlier reputation she had earned as a mad mother cow, because the rules were different. Millie's calf could walk alongside her in the arena, so she again behaved like a dream while earning her purple ribbons as Bonner County's finest Hereford cow.

Good behavior aside, Millie eventually served as the cata-
lyst for an event that would revive Bob Nesbitt's warnings about
"those horns" and prove his admonitions true. One day "those
horns" nearly disemboweled me. The offending horns belonged
to another of Millie's sons, named Billy. Millie's behavior lapses
had been limited to those moments when her calf was missing,
but Billy had no concept of good behavior from the start. This
young bull had it in for humans. Hours of standing in a box stall
tied to a manger full of hay and grain did nothing to quiet his
snorts or dirty looks. Billy just plain didn't like people.

We finally decided that such an ungrateful creature could
grace someone else's farm. Billy's pedigree appeared in the February bull sale catalog the year he turned two. Animals sold at
this sale had to be halter-broke and fitted just as we did for the
fair. One January day I got Billy into the barn to start grooming
him. To keep him distracted, I filled the grain box and loaded up
the manger with hay before getting the brushes and curry comb.

I had not been in the stall more than ten seconds when
Billy decided he needed his space and I was invading it. Glaring
and snorting, he came at me with his head down, intent on hitting his mark. He did. My reflexes had forgotten to get up that
day. I stood motionless as Billy smacked me—literally head on—
in the stomach and rammed me up against the wall. My only
salvation was the heavy winter coat that softened the blow and
somehow doubled as a hornproof stomach protector. I don't know
how long I was pinned to the wall, but I do know how fast I
climbed it once Billy let go for an instant to plan his second
move. Outside the barn, I gathered my wits and what remained
of my coat. The coat was never the same again, nor was my
attitude about horned Herefords. Bob Nesbitt was right. those
critters would look a lot better without their blasted horns.

Billy went to the sale without a lot of tender-loving care
from me. His reputation became known countywide the instant

he came down the chute from Harold's truck. Everyone knew Billy had arrived. It was obvious this animal had hit his terrible twos. He threw tantrums. He threatened to butt anyone who so much as looked at him, let alone came near his stall. When his number came up, the cattlemen opened the gate and carefully encouraged him to the sale ring. As he entered the small enclosure, the ring men exited by way of the nearest fence. Like the bulls in Pamplona, Spain, Billy galloped around, stopping occasionally to paw the shavings and hurl them wildly into the air over his back. He glared at the audience with an expression that belligerently dared any mortal to take him on.

No one chose to take Billy home that day. Not one bid was offered.

When bidding closed, someone in the crowd kept Billy's attention as another brave soul ran for the door leading to the stock pens, flung it open, and scaled the fence just in time for the bull to discover the opening and vanish from view. The problem was that Billy also managed to vanish from the stockyard. Exploding through the aisle between the pens, the mad beast bypassed an open gate to an empty stall and bullied his way though the aisle maze, sending the stockyard gallery scrambling for safety. One group of cattlemen had been opening a gate that led to the outside world when Billy's rampage had sent them running for cover. Billy pushed the gate wide open and galloped for freedom, snorting and bellowing across the sale yard parking lot. While the auctioneer attempted to maintain order in the sale area, Harold and several other cattlemen hot-footed it outside and began pursuit—some on foot, some in trucks. Heading north, Billy had already reached the road before Harold managed to jump into his cattle truck and turn it around for the chase.

Thundering through front yards and along ditches, Billy eventually reached Highway 95, almost a mile away from the sale yard. Rather than head straight across the highway, which would lead him home, Billy chose to go toward Canada, where he could possibly lead the life of an illegal alien. Dodging semis and other Saturday morning traffic, he romped about half a mile down the highway before Harold passed him with the cattle truck, jumped out with lariat in hand, and miraculously intimidated him into someone's driveway. Harold's Montana cowboy talents came into play as he twirled his lariat noose, sent it flying, and scored a direct hit on Billy's horns. Quickly snubbing the insane beast to a conveniently located fencepost, Harold held on with all his might until the rest of the posse arrived.

The group eventually got crazy Billy back into the truck and back to the sale yard, where they locked him in a pen. Anytime anyone had the nerve to walk by his pen or the audacity to lay eyes on him, Billy issued threats, snorting or digging holes in the ground. The naughty bull stayed at the saleyard for three weeks before some feedlot owner bought him for beef. We always wondered about the poor souls who had to eat Billy burgers.

My experience with Billy taught me a healthy respect for the potential of a mad bull with horns. The next winter my desire to work with "great horned cows" fully disintegrated when I met another one head-on. Mary Elephant had moved to our ranch as a yearling. Mother and Harold had purchased her from Howard and Mary Ellen Thomason, who owned the Selkirk Ranch, north of Sandpoint. Years before, they had started a small herd in their backyard on Cedar Street. They had taken it from the back lot in the city limits to the country where they built one of the most beautiful ranches in Bonner County. Their Selkirk line of Herefords garnered national fame. In spite of their success, Howard and Mary Ellen kept a very personal touch with their "lovely cows." Mary Ellen loved each one as if it were a child, just as she did her thirty-plus cats, giving every living critter on the Selkirk Ranch a name. However, when my folks went out to purchase a big yearling heifer from the Thomasons, Mary Ellen had slipped behind on her personalized approach. So we decided to name our new heifer after Mary Ellen, who was flattered.

The problem was, Mary Ellen—the cow—grew, and grew, and grew, like the beanstalk. Almost everything on Mary Ellen grew, especially her face. As she turned three, she stood more than five feet at the shoulders. The taller she grew, the lower her face stretched toward the ground. It was as if her mouth were too heavy, causing the bone structure to continually extend. Two parts of her anatomy that failed to grow were her horns and her eyes, which in no way matched the proportions of her long, homely face. Her tiny little eyes looked like miniature black pebbles amidst the white, and her stubby little horns projected out about an inch before curling back toward her head. The huge cow with the long, deadpan face would never be a "Heifer of the Month" foldout in the *Hereford Journal*.

She didn't seem like a Mary Ellen, either. Mary Ellen Thomason was a refined, well-educated lady from illustrious Southern bloodlines. The cow probably had good bloodlines, too, but that was as far as the similarity went. So one day we opted for a name change. From that day forth, our large cow was known, more appropriately, as Mary Elephant.

From the time she arrived at our place, Mary Elephant had been a timid cow, never too interested in making friends, but one who never minded people either. At least until one January day after she had just given birth, when I had the misfortune to once again learn about cows and their maternal instincts. We rarely had baby calves in January because of the cold, snow, ice, and drizzle. For some reason, Mary Elephant hadn't followed the ranch's usual mating schedule. After discovering her new calf in the barnyard, Harold came in to get his syringe and vaccine. It was his standard policy to vaccinate calves against a killer disease called white muscle. Hearing that there was a new baby outside, I wasted no time getting my duds on to inspect it. Harold had gone ahead and was preparing to give the calf a shot as I slid through the gate. The ground was covered with a thick sheet of ice, and it had rained the night before, leaving the barnyard an obstacle course patterned with hundreds of icy, water-filled depressions.

Carefully choosing each step, I made my way toward Mary Elephant. At first she paid no heed, but when I slid to a mere fifteen feet away, she put her head down and looked me in the eye as if to say, "I wouldn't come any closer if I were you."

I must have been dense that morning, because I did not take the hint. I took another step. That's when Mary Elephant sent me a more direct message to leave her territory. Her head went down, her tail in the air, and her body into action. Surprisingly surefooted, she came running at me. For a brief second I stood paralyzed with disbelief, then, coming to my senses, I turned to run the other way. Ice puddles conspired with the cow. I got about three feet before falling flat on my face. I looked up to see Mary Elephant still coming, her ugly little horns suddenly resembling devil's spikes. I looked down and saw my only defense: besides water, the puddles were filled with ample supplies of cow droppings.

Self-preservation destroys childish squeamishness. Grabbing a gob of the frozen slop, I flung it into the air toward Mary Elephant and screamed, "Get out of here, you creep!" Lucky for me, Mary Elephant crumbled at the sight of the slop and the sound of an insulting name. She stopped dead in her tracks, then turned around and went back to her calf, where she stood issuing silent threats with that pathetic face. After picking myself up, I decided it best to honor Mary Elephant's wishes and check out the calf on another day. Dripping with barnyard slop, I slid back to the house and removed half my filthy, wet clothes before going inside to clean up.

My close call, coupled with the Billy blow-up, sealed it for me. Bob Nesbitt was right: A cow with no horns could be a kinder, gentler cow.

FOOT COVER-UPS
That FAILED

I envy people with beautiful feet.

Some might chide me, saying, "Oh, Marianne, the toes always grow prettier on the other foot." But I've got a clear-cut case for wishing we could shed toes as easily as we get rid of that first set of teeth. With my luck, though, the toe fairy would refuse to pay up if he/she ever found one of my pinkies under a pillow. If a podiatrist ever dreams up a cosmetic cure for ugly

feet, I'll be first in line for a foot lift, with a set of hoof nippers and a heavy-duty rasp to chisel away the jagged mountains jutting from my big toes.

For years, my feet have provided insensitive friends and family members the inspiration for their—ahem—lame humor. One such experience made me particularly sensitive. On a July afternoon spent soaking up some sun at Lake Pend Oreille's Sam Owen Campground near Hope, Idaho, my mother started critiquing the quarter-inch-thick nails on my two big toes. "Those are the strangest toenails I've ever seen. Look at those things!" she exclaimed, loudly enough for half the beach to hear.

My mother's penchant for total honesty has often conflicted with her less enthusiastic zest for tact. I immediately dug all ten digits into the sand, refusing to expose them again until she had walked back to the car.

Now, when it comes to her own feet, Mother is more than slightly narcissistic. With a superior air, she has often praised her lovely feet. Her conceit could be a defense mechanism in reaction to our merciless appraisal of her "purebred" nose. An unknown scientific authority once told someone in our family that snout size directly corresponds with the purity of one's bloodlines. None of us has been blessed with a cute button nose, and Mother's nasal protuberance leads the pack of prominent proboscises within our family. We have always delighted in launching cruel nose jokes her way, so her "callous" evaluation of my toes that day was retaliation I deserved.

Sadly, another summer outing reemphasized my need for foot cover-ups. A group of my former yearbook students invited me to a swimming party, and we all gathered on the dock to swap experiences and reminisce. Jeffrey, a normally thoughtful soul who has continued to send me May Day flowers ever since his sophomore year in 1981, shot a glance at my bare feet, stared a few seconds, then made me want to shoot myself (in the foot, of course). "Mrs. Love, where did you get those toenails?" he blurted. "Everyone, look at her toenails! They're like granite!"

Everyone obliged.

Once more I cringed and ran. For the rest of that afternoon, I wore my socks in the water as well as out. The sheer embarrassment of having my special students discover this imperfection in their honored teacher was more than I could bear. From that time forward, I have never been seen at public beaches without socks or shoes to hide my terrible tootsies. Only immediate family have managed brief and unwelcome toe-sightings as I've scurried through the house in search of a clean pair of socks. If my relatives insensitively comment and hurt my feelings once more, I may have to invest in some sort of permanent toenail covers—possibly the Lee's Press-On variety.

Foot fear haunts me when I think about my final day. The morticians will wheel my cadaver into the morgue, attach an identification tag to my big toe, then collapse with laughter. My mother always instructed me to wear clean underwear in case of an accident, murder, or any other form of premature death. But my phobia about being caught with soiled undies comes nowhere near my paranoia about having folks snicker at my corpse's ten terrible tootsies.

It's no wonder my unsightly feet will never be selected to model for a Madison Avenue ad agency. Foot abuse was a common malady among us Brown children. Like other kids in the 1950s, we suffered occasional agony from stepping on our share of rusty nails lurking in the deep grass on our forty-acre North Boyer farm. I'll never forget the perverse delight I once experienced after cutting my arch with a piece of glass amid the rubble in the woodshed. The glass apparently pierced a blood vessel; every time I took a step my foot functioned like a pump. Long streams of deep, red blood arched upward at least four feet in the air. It was a wonderful phenomenon. I entertained ideas of marketing the act, but the blood soon clotted, bringing my talent to a close as quickly as it had been discovered.

Actually, running around barefoot and encountering hidden hazards was the least of our foot problems. The real demons fell into four categories: stinking shoes, shrinking shoes, suffering (alias "cruel") shoes, and talking shoes.

Stinking shoes picked certain times of the year to erupt. My two brothers and I were oblivious to the fact that running around barefoot then slipping into a pair of sneakers in mid-August was and is a deadly combination. We three seldom devoted time to scrubbing toe jam and scraping the barnyard crud off the soles of our feet, and spent even less time searching for clean, matching socks. If we did wear them, the socks were related to the famed ABC gum of the early 1960s—they were known as ABWST's (Already Been Worn Several Times).

The odor of my faulty socks rarely affected me as much as it did my other unsuspecting nasal victims. After all, I was used to my bodily emissions and rather enjoyed my personal aroma. But when I shed the shoes in confined areas, the reactions of my folks and my equally pungent but critical big brothers led to diatribes that would make Saddam Hussein's look like a choir boy's.

"What just died?" they'd moan, or, "Get those (deleted) feet out of here!!" The remarks made me squirm, but my sense of logic at that age rarely matched my family's collective sense of smell. If only I had been as innovative as one of my friend's brothers, who put his stinky feet to use in the family television room. He had a simple strategy for getting to watch whatever show he wanted: removing his shoes, he sent his siblings scrambling within seconds.

Besides horrifying family members with our obnoxious odors, Mike, Kevin, and I exasperated our folks with the mysterious shrinking shoe syndrome. We seemed to have an uncanny ability to stretch our shoe sizes by several millimeters each month. "Marianne has already grown out of those shoes I bought her just three weeks ago," my mother sputtered several times yearly. Her remarks did several psychological numbers on me when I was a kid, and paired with my guilty Catholic conscience had quite an impact. Believe me, I attempted numerous methods for stopping sinful foot growth, but no matter what I did, my feet spread like pie dough at the mercy of a rolling pin.

Harold's City Water Department paycheck unfortunately failed to grow proportionately with our feet, so whipping on down to Del's Family Shoe Store on First Avenue in Sandpoint wasn't possible every time our feet cried out for space. We had to suffer. Toes weathered the storm by doubling over and digging into insoles. More often than not, my little toe refused to conform, rebelliously bursting through the side of my shoe much like a baby robin bursting from its egg. When this happened, cause and effect ruled that my socks would pick up permanent stains on their outside edges. We could invariably count on six months in the same footgear, which naturally led to a little wear and tear here and there. Thus spawning the third North Boyer footwear phenomenon: cruel—maybe even sadistic—shoes.

Generally, the most vulnerable part of my shoe was the heel. After wearing down on the outside, causing several close calls with sprained ankles or the humiliating sudden sidewalk stumble syndrome, my long-worn shoes plotted their ultimate revenge: their heels would either threaten to fall off or, demonically, drop by the wayside when I least expected it. If I were lucky enough to retrieve a fallen heel, I reattached it with a nail or two. Since Harold's junk drawer seldom contained nails short enough for quarter-inch heels, and since earlier attempts with thumb tacks had failed, I rounded off the naked nail tips to avoid scratching linoleum or gym floors. I usually pounded them in the other way, though, so was doomed to deal with the sharp projectiles that poked their ways up through the insole, causing relentless pressure and excruciating pain at every step. To stop the pain, I applied Band-Aid bandages or folded-up Kleenex tissues to the back of the insole. Many times I still lacked the padding necessary to escape that piercing poke, so I walked around on my tiptoes, a North Idaho geisha girl in jeans. Such foot misery kept me on my toes throughout childhood.

With the passing of years, I had all but forgotten another aspect of footgear that set my brothers and me apart from our classmates. Mike's first grade class picture, taken on the steps of Lincoln School, brought it all back. As children, we thanked our ancestors for having the foresight to match genes with tall folks; we never got stuck in the front row for class photos. But my own second grade picture shows that row position didn't solve the shoe problem. In it, Patricia Rash sits demurely in the front row. It's easy to focus on her feet because they don't yet touch the pavement of the school steps. Her black-and-white saddle shoes are secured with clean, white laces, and her alabaster anklets are neatly cuffed. In her adorable ruffled skirt, Patricia sits cute as a little bug's ear amid such notables as Larry Copley and Vance Ekwortzell. Immediately behind her slouches Marianne Brown in her plaid jumper and white blouse. It's apparent that Marianne is attempting to hide her feet directly behind David Harney's lace-up clodhoppers. Unfortunately, the ploy has failed—it's hard to miss Marianne's large, scuffed oxfords and droopy socks between Maria Sanner's spotlessly white tennis shoes and Kathleen Brackney's spiffy black patent sandals.

Our shoes rarely made positive fashion statements, but they did speak on many occasions. As each school year wore on and our footwear wore out, we came to class in "talking" shoes, which announced to all that Mike, Kevin, and Marianne were unfortunate souls whose soles had chosen to separate from the rest of their shoes. Folks could hear us flopping into any room. To make matters worse for us, toe jam reigned supreme as dust, sand, sawdust, sticks and rocks found their way into the gaping scoop-shovels on our feet. Again we used ingenuity, salvaging what was left of our pride and those unfortunate flappers by using rubber bands to keep our soles under control. Our strategy lessened the noise, but we still suffered the sensation of "something lost, something gained" with every step we took.

Probably more than any other influence, those talking shoes impressed upon me the importance of a college education. Get that degree. Start a career. Escape from poverty and never again be too poor to purchase shoes whenever you need them. Better yet, spare your own children the humiliation of having people stare and glare at their feet. Never would my kids need to hide in the back rows when school portrait day came. And never would that smell, reminiscent of Limburger cheese, permeate my house.

I got the degree, married the husband. Our two-income family has two kids, two dogs, two horses—and closets full of shoes. However, I have learned that talking, shrinking, stinking, and suffering shoes occur regardless of family financial status. Oh, sure, we can and do replace offending footgear more quickly than my folks could. But I've gotten strangely nostalgic watching Annie slip her crusty toes out of her filthy Reeboks. And Willie can clear a room when he takes off his $150 Air Jordans, just as I could when I undid my beat-up sneakers.

Why MOTHER'S CUPBOARD *Went* BARE

It's been almost thirty years since I lived at my childhood home, yet I still haven't broken the habit of looking for goodies in Mother's refrigerator every time I enter her house on North Boyer.

For years, the family Frigidaire resided just inside her kitchen under a nest of baseball caps, beat-up western hats, and mismatched work gloves. It came to our house back when I was in the first grade in 1953-54 after having served for several years keeping milk cartons cold at Northside Elementary School. And it faithfully housed the Tibbs produce until Christmas 1993, when my brother Mike and his wife decided to surprise the folks with a new General Electric model. Working toward its fifth decade of being cool, Mother and Harold's loyal fridge will live

out the rest of its days in the barnyard tack shed, keeping pop cold for my sisters' riding students.

Having withstood countless grimy hands poking around at its contents, the refrigerator deserves an award for service above and beyond the appliance call of duty. It could win the Purple Ice Cube award for setting thirteen world records in "Number of Months Endured Before Being Defrosted." I can remember times when the ice cube shelves had no definable shape, their metal walls and dividers having disappeared into five inches of hard-packed snowdrifts. Mother cannot. "We could always get ice out of the top tray," she claims. I'll stand by my story. I clearly remember prying those first ice trays out when lemonade time came in June. The job always challenged my patience and sometimes led to bloody injury. Pounding on the butcher knife to chip away at the square igloo was awkward at best. Occasionally the knife slipped, stabbing my nearest body part.

When she opened the fridge door and spotted someone else's amateur snow sculpture in the upper compartment, Mother finally decided it was time to defrost. As an adult appliance owner, I know why she put it off so long. Defrosting meant emptying double-digit amounts of rotten, soggy, moldy, mysterious, crusted, drippy, slimy, hardened, smelly, sticky, and just plain strange concoctions. It strained the senses and filled observers with wonder to see the smorgasbord of well-aged delectables take over the entire kitchen counter. We kids avoided the kitchen when Mother started defrosting since her mood on the job was never good; the ominous comments and strange noises she made while selectively removing and evaluating items intimidated us. Over time we grew wise enough to get involved in some time-consuming project far, far away from the house. We had seen the refrigerator flea market often enough to know that the Frigidaire's capacity and Mother's patience maxed out simultaneously, and outgrew the need to hear Mother invent new expletives as she chipped away at petrified tuna fish and dumped pregnant cellophane bags (which threatened to go into labor) into the overflowing trash can.

I'm amazed that so many food items remained in the Tibbs family refrigerator long enough to decompose into alienlike entities. In their first batch of kids, Mother and Harold molded three of the best eaters in Bonner County. Three good farm meals a day with ample portions and multiple courses never quite satisfied our need for more . . . and more. We were always hungry.

Unlike other families like our close friends the Crocketts, whose household had no laws against guzzling an extra carton of milk or a cookie anytime they wanted one, we three were under strict consumption regulations. We loathed going into town to the Crocketts' house because, while Mother and Helen Crockett visited, Helen's son Robert would blithely open their fridge, grab a quart of Darigold ice cream, and top it off with a handful of cookies. Only after dinner, when a plate of cookies—carefully counted out to allow two apiece—circled the living room, were we allowed such goodies.

Taking food between meals was a crime at our house, but we became willing criminals. Our methods surpassed those of the slickest burglars, but the banks we heisted included the refrigerator, the cupboards, the freezer, and the padlocked vault known as the fruit room. Mother attempted more than one *Mission: Impossible* to control our theft, but each of her security schemes only whetted our appetites. If we three had gone into crime instead of our chosen careers in toilet-paper-tycooning, forestry, or teaching, Mother would have provided us with the most sophisticated challenges for perfecting our craft.

Our pilfering usually occurred when Mother went to the barn for chores or to the Boyer Store to buy more groceries. I estimate that during our childhood years approximately 1,239 slices of Wonder Bread disappeared while Mother was out of the house. Another 339 vanished when she was in the living room watching soap operas or talking on the telephone, and another 47 found their illicit ways into our stomachs when she was actually in the kitchen. Mike and Kevin perfected their method of absconding with bread slices to the point that each could silently open the drawer, select a slice, stuff it under his shirt, and slide the drawer shut while Mother stirred gravy at the stove, just five feet away. They were developing a technique for gobbling their take without leaving the kitchen, but Mike's high school graduation and appointment to West Point took him away before they had a chance to test it.

Bread theft took on different dimensions, depending on Mother's proximity to the crime in progress. If she was in the kitchen, only one slice disappeared at a time. The thief put it under his shirt, then slipped out of the kitchen and into his bedroom, where he consumed it in two or three bites. If she was in the living room the tactics remained the same but the number of slices increased—averaging three on those occasions. If Mother was outside or, better yet, in town, an additional procedure accompanied the theft. Coating each slice with a layer of sugar, my brothers and I stacked one on top of another and wadded the collection up in a ball. We bit into the mass only after it had been molded and packed solidly. We three could never enjoy these treats at the same time, however, because creating wads required too many slices of bread. We had the decency to consider the effect on Mother's blood pressure if she discovered that a loaf she purchased in the morning had only two slices remaining by lunch time.

I recall one awful morning when my thievery nearly did me in. I was alone in the kitchen. The boys had gone somewhere. Harold was at work at the filter plant. Mother was out in the barn brushing her horse. "I've got time to make a peanut butter sandwich," I muttered quietly to myself.

Peeking through the porch window, I spied Mother leading her Arab mare Cricket to the barn. It was safe. Grabbing slices of bread, the butter plate, and the jar of peanut butter, I worked quickly, spreading the contents, putting everything away, and brushing the crumbs from the counter. As I finished, I looked out the kitchen window and spotted Mother coming around the woodshed toward the house.

I wasted no time looking for cover. With sandwich stuffed into the top of my pants and covered up with my shirt, I dashed to the bathroom. Once securely behind the door, I began to destroy the evidence by chomping off huge bites and chewing each no more than two times apiece. Hearing the back door open, I hurried this process along, bypassing chewing and just coaxing the bread and peanut butter mixture down my throat.

Don't ever try to hurry peanut butter.

The kitchen door opened and closed as I was attempting to swallow half of the sandwich at once. "Marianne?" Mother called. I flushed the toilet to buy time. The stubborn mass lodged in my throat, blocking off all passages. I could neither spit nor swallow. "Marianne, are you in there?" she inquired once more. I flushed again, still trying to swallow. The glob remained firmly in place. "Marianne, why do you keep flushing the toilet? What are you doing in there?"

"Mmoogmmooghmoogh—moomgh," was all I could manage as the lump pushed against my glottis, distorting any coherent sounds I attempted.

Trying to interpret my response from the other side of the door, Mother asked, "What did you say? I can't understand what you said."

I knew a second mumbled response would give me away, so like a Lamaze coach I called on all my throat muscles to bear down for one final push of the peanut butter glob. I had my first hint of the experience of hard labor as the peanutty mass finally let loose and slipped down my throat—not without pain and the permanent conviction that I would never get in this fix again. Free at last, I cast aside all my discomfort and yelled back my usual response to her curious questions. "Nothing," I blurted, "Just going to the toilet."

"Well, hurry up and get out of there," she ordered, moving on toward the living room. Her departure and absence of suspicion gave me time to safely dispose of the remaining sandwich without choking to death in the process. I reveled in the fact that my coming unglued from the peanut butter had also saved my mother from coming unglued herself.

The scene was never pretty when Mother discovered food missing. Any kid who happened to be within earshot—guilty or not—endured her fury. She never did figure out that the guilty party was probably not going to be lounging around waiting for punishment. One day she pulled open the bread drawer to discover that the bag of Nalley's potato chips she had purchased two hours earlier had a mysterious rip in the side seam and precisely eighty-nine fewer chips.

"Okay! Who took these chips?" she sputtered. "We were going to eat these with our hamburgers tonight. Who took them????"

"Twasn't me," was the response from all of us who sprawled innocently in their chairs nearby. "I didn't even know there were any chips." Feigned innocence/ignorance was always impressive.

Mother's mood failed to improve. "I can't have anything without kids getting their grimy hands into it," she moaned while sticking sesame seed buns on top of fat, juicy hamburgers sizzling in the frying pan. "Everybody will have to suffer tonight because there are hardly any chips left for supper." The litany expanded with her indignation as she flew around the kitchen grabbing ketchup, mustard, and Miracle Whip sandwich spread, slamming the jars on the table. "I'm not going to buy any chips anymore!" she threatened. "Why can't you pigs stay out of the food?" Mother's anger over stolen potato chips and other delectables could turn even the most innocent, squeaky clean conscience black with sin. Someone suffered the consequences, even if that someone had not so much as a crystal of potato chip salt on his or her tongue.

Mother learned to reinforce her guilt-producing abilities with physical proof—she set traps for the thieves. Besides carefully placing cookies in specified patterns and memorizing the exact folds of aluminum foil on each cake pan, she occasionally sacrificed some of her precious food to teach us children object lessons, convincing us of our folly in thinking we could get away with even crumbs of the family food supply. Once, after Sunday Mass, she was preparing the usual pot roast, potatoes, and carrots as Mike, Kevin, and I sat around the kitchen table exchanging the usual stupid smart remarks. "Who would like a cookie?" she suddenly offered, stretching her arm above her five-foot-two frame to reach the Tudor-style cookie jar on top of the water heater.

"I do!"

"I do!"

Two out of three chirped almost in perfect unison, but Kevin had failed to join our chorus. "I don't!" he barked.

"Why don't you want any cookies, Kevin?" Mother asked sarcastically. "These are delicious chocolate no-bake cookies. I thought you liked them." She walked toward the table, lifting the chimney and the roof from the ceramic house of goodies. "You're not eating any cookies? That's not like you, Kevin," she continued. "Are you sick?"

Mike and I were both amazed as Kevin once more declined the rare opportunity to have a cookie. But Kevin and Mother both knew something that we didn't.

Standing above us, a triumphant gleam on her face, she

pressed on. "What's the matter, Kevin? Do you know something about these cookies? Why don't you want one? Look, they're delicious." She presented the container for inspection.

Mother had pulled off a crime-detecting ploy surely never attempted at any other household across the United States. She had no doubt laughed fiendishly while placing those ten cookies in the bottom of the cookie jar and sprinkling them with cayenne pepper. As we viewed the red powder on top of the cookies, it was obvious that the red-faced thief had been caught red-handed. Kevin had sampled her new spicy recipe and decided thumbs-down on second helpings.

Mother's success was short-lived, since she had raised kids with resilience and brilliance to match her own. We three older kids continued to outwit her and screw up her meal planning. We drank dill pickle juice straight from the jar after stealing the last pickle. We practiced finger painting on chocolate cakes. Even the freezer wasn't safe; we soon learned that a butcher knife slipped in between the lid and the main part of the freezer could push the lock out of its slot with ease. Kevin took great pride in showing Mike and me his discovery one day, and from that time on nothing good was safe inside the family Coldspot. Well, some things were—Mike caught a seventeen-inch cutthroat trout in Sand Creek that resided safely in the freezer for about ten years along with some packages of venison chops from one of Harold's deer. But ice cream had a freezer life of maybe a day.

We food thieves loved December, when Mother baked at least thirty kinds of Christmas treats and stuffed them away in freezer canisters and aluminum foil. I remember the Christmas Eve when Mother began preparing the cookie plates she traditionally took to friends, then discovered that the contents of several freezer containers had dwindled dramatically. Her verbal explosions rocked the house and convinced us we would be wise to limit our pilfering during the next year's baking marathon

Bad as we were, we had the decency to realize that our thievery had ruined Mother's generous plans to help others.

The frozen food theft with the most startling result occurred one summer when Mike and Kevin had branched out into bigger, more exciting games—like fishing. Sand Creek no longer satisfied their adventurous spirit; they looked for lunkers on the shores of Lake Pend Oreille. Having heard the tales about world famous Kamloops trout that anglers reeled in from the lake's waters, my brothers wanted to add their names to the fishing hall of fame. Through deductive reasoning, the boys figured that if an angleworm would catch a twelve-inch cutthroat, bigger bait should lure a forty-pound Kamloops. After considering several possibilities, they finally agreed on the perfect plan for luring the world's biggest trout. No greedy Kamloops could resist the temptation to swim up and sample the most exotic culinary delight known to man and fish: a well-marbled sirloin steak.

Early one morning, butcher knife at the ready, the boys pilfered the key to their immortality as North Idaho fishing legends. A quick slip of the knife and they were on their way to the lake with fishing poles and four frozen steaks from Mother's freezer. The boys never did make national fishing expert Babe Winkleman's honor roll, but they did reel in some award-winning two-legged suckers, of the out-of-town variety. They already had their lines in the water when some tourists came along the shore. Knowing an opportunity when he saw it, Kevin decided to put on a show for the intruding anglers. "I got one," he hollered, reeling in. The pole began to bend as he guided his line. "This is a big one!"

The visitors stopped to stare as Kevin's pole, manipulated to look like the "lunker" was putting up quite a fight, bent nearly in two. His audience closed in.

"Wow, this is a record!" Kevin exclaimed as the drama of

the slow-moving lunker kept the crowd entranced. Slowly, carefully, he brought in line as the tip of the pole nearly touched the water. Just as the spectators knew they were about to lay eyes on the biggest, most spectacular trout ever landed on the shoreline of that North Idaho lake, Kevin stomped his feet and squawked, "Oh no! It got away!" His expression was heavy. His audience sighed sympathetically. The drama waned—until Kevin reeled in the last of his line. The steak, a bit limp and soaked to the gills, hung from the pole. "Oh well, I still have my bait," he commented. Jaws gaping like large-mouthed bass, the visitors retreated, shaking their heads in amazement. More than likely they surmised that a trip to the nearest supermarket meat department, where they could purchase the secret to North Idaho fishing, was in order.

When Kevin shared this tale at the dinner table years later, Mother's reaction was tempered by the passage of time. She had become resigned to the fact that our dark past included some rather strange episodes. During another of these confessions, Mother learned why her egg supply had diminished so dramatically on numerous unexplained occasions.

While other teenagers cruised the beach on hot summer nights, Kevin, Susie Baldwin, and I had found other amusements. Mother's eggs had provided the yoke, if you'll forgive the pun. Loading up about a dozen or so in a brown paper bag and disappearing quietly from the house, Kevin and I met Susie at a prearranged site to decide which neighbor's cows would get that night's egg bath. There was something unmistakably thrilling about hitting a bovine target literally head-on and watching gooey yolk and egg white dribble slowly down the bemused animal's face. One time we were almost caught hurling our messy ammunition into neighbors' barnyard and had to hide in a chicken house for half an hour as our victims' owner suddenly showed up on his John Deere tractor. During our great escape that evening through the swamps near Sand Creek, I fell behind when my shoes got stuck in the mud. By the time I retrieved them Kevin and Susie were long gone, so I had to hobble home alone. I haven't forgiven them.

Mother was a bit more horrified hearing about her eggs, almost as horrified as she had been years earlier when Harold discovered the remains of many of her home canned goods, along with some of her silverware, in the woods. Clearing and burning brush one summer, Harold decided to remove several hollow stumps. Sawing away, he found that two stumps were doubling as dump sites. At the bottom of each sat an empty quart jar containing a tablespoon. His initial discovery sent Harold on a stump inspection tour, yielding half a dozen Kerr canning jars and five spoons.

Kevin was the culprit. He enjoyed sitting under the trees and spooning in quart-sized helpings of pears, peaches, and applesauce. Sometimes in need of a quick fruit fix, he simply walked in the pantry, shut the door, and stood among the shelves and sacks of dry goods, shoveling in bite after bite of home-canned fruit. Occasionally he got interrupted or decided to save a few peach halves for later. Rather than polishing off the jar contents, he left it and its remaining contents in the fruit room. Eventually, Mother noticed that her beautiful rows of canned goods seemed different from when she had proudly placed them on the shelf. It dawned on her that the fruit was not simply going through the normal shrinkage that occurs after canning. On closer inspection, she could see that the seal to the lids had been broken and that a thief had, indeed, left his sticky evidence upon the shelves.

Comparing notes and compiling several pages of evidence, Mother and Harold chose Kevin as their prime suspect. They decided to make an example of him one night at the dinner table when dessert time arrived. Rather than rich chocolate, that evening's offering was a dish of pears for each person at the table—except Kevin. Confident that their plan would effectively convince him to stay out of Mother's fruit supply forever, she placed a quart jar in front of him, telling him to enjoy it down to the last pear. Totally oblivious to her intentions and without so much as a sigh, Kevin followed instructions to the letter. The entire family watched with amazement as he ate away, displaying no awareness that he was being punished. With the last spoonful of syrup, he looked up with a satisfied grin and asked, "Are there seconds?"

And so it was—a childhood of kids stealing, Mother setting traps, kids outwitting her. The cycle continued until we moved out and founded homes of our own. I have grown to understand my mother's frustration better and better while watching brand new jars of Nalley's banquet dills disappear within hours of purchase, or when grabbing for a pop tart only to find an empty box and a wad of silver wrappers. It's a thankless job raising human pigs. Still, there is some solace knowing they, too, will raise hungry families of their own.

POCKET GIRDLES

Throughout her childhood my mother attended Catholic boarding schools where stern nuns taught her to be a lady. She thought she could do the same for me.

Mother failed.

Her inability to bequeath those refined ways to her daughter might have stemmed from the fact that she tried too hard. Or it might be that my rough and tough Irish genes overwhelmed her sophisticated English and French bloodlines. Whatever the cause, Mother's offspring were throwbacks to something more primitive than she could have envisioned.

I started out all right. During my days in the crib or those as an angelic little toddler, I could charm anyone with my big, beaming brown eyes and innocent little grin. My adorable chiffon dresses accented with ruffles showed fine taste. My nicely

Douglas mansion manistee mi.

formed bald head had its own charm, and the coils of auburn locks that sprang forth from it in my first year only added to my appeal. My future looked bright. It was generally thought I would follow in my mother's footsteps and grow up into a sophisticated young lady.

In spite of her hard work and training. Mother encountered many a detour in the road to refinement—her route ultimately turned into a dead end. I don't know exactly when Mother threw in the towel, but I can vividly remember some experiences that certainly alerted her to the fact that her eldest daughter would never pass for royal stock.

The public school system supported her efforts for years by requiring that girls wear dresses to school every day. On the day I started first grade at Lincoln School she took special pains to see that I left the house spit-shined, fully groomed, and properly dressed. She bought me a pretty dress with the frilly ruffles and rounded me up the night before to do a job on my hair. I learned to hate the eves of special occasions such as school programs or birthday parties or visits from my grandmother since Mother chose those times to do battle on my scalp. Armed with the weaponry of long, skinny scraps of white cotton, comb, glass of water, and aggressive fingers, she directed me to a chair next to the kitchen table. I plopped down and hunched over, attempting to assume a seated fetal position as she hovered over me grabbing gobs of hair to slick down with water from the glass. Next came a finger lock so snug that it threatened to detach an entire batch of roots. Inserting a rag at the top of the section she carefully applied the mummy wrap until not a hair could be seen. I held my head perfectly still so that I wouldn't spoil her intricate handiwork. Her grip offered me no choice but to cooperate fully, lest I learn firsthand about real scalpings of naughty little girls. The rag headdress usually took about half an hour to fashion.

Done up in such a way, I looked like an alien cousin of the Statue of Liberty. Anyone who saw me surely would have liked to add a torch to the scene—by lighting each of the roll-your-owns that stuck out all over my head. It was bad enough looking at myself in the mirror, but when I tried to sleep on my giant quills I had to invent new ways to count sheep. Usually I opted to sleep face down, my nose ground into the pillow. Smothering seemed much more desirable than tossing and turning to avoid the scalp stretching and poking of my curlers.

The object of the rag operation, according to Mother, was the enhancement of my already naturally curly hair. She loved hearing people remark, "What pretty hair Marianne has!" If the natural "do" got attention, think what ringlets would evoke!

I did not share my mother's enthusiasm for having people dote over my hair. In fact, I still shudder to recall the day when Gertrude Racicot and her daughter Catherine instructed me to pose so they could marvel over my hair. "Stand over there in the sun," Gertrude said at a summer picnic. "We want to see it shine through your hair." When you're five you do what adults tell you, so I obediently stepped into a streak of sunlight. "Now turn around and look this way," she instructed. Gertrude, one of the pillars of the local Presbyterian church, was a tall, slender monument of a woman who always appeared to be dressed to go listen to a Sunday sermon. She also appeared to be about eighty-five years old. I think she was in a time warp because she stayed eighty-five for the next thirty or so years.

That day I performed the obligatory stance in the sun, elderly Gertrude leaned toward Catherine and beheld my hair. "Oh, look at it," she beamed. "Isn't it lovely? The sun brings out the red in it."

Those were fighting words. Gertrude had said my hair was red.

"I don't have red hair," I sullenly told myself. For some

unknown reason, when I was five I hated red hair. It may have had something to do with my red-headed big brother who didn't always treat me right. I could not and would not accept the notion that I had even one strand of red hair on my head—my hair was brown! Standing in the hot sun hearing such offensive remarks was almost more than I could take. But Gertrude meant no harm. Her well-meaning admiration of my curly locks simply reinforced Mother's determination to give me a rag-do the night before I entered Lincoln School for the first time.

Between the discomfort of having to sleep with my nose buried in the pillow, I didn't get much sleep. I instinctively knew that too much time without oxygen could do me in, and on that night I did not want that to happen. I had stood at the end of the driveway too many times watching my brothers board the school bus—wishing just once I could sneak along. I wanted to go to school so badly that I thought someone might feel sorry for me and say, "Oh, come on, Marianne. Get on the bus. You can go to school today." But it never happened. I had to wait for the right birthday to make it all possible. So when September 1953 finally came, I was not going to let the danger of smothering to death in my pillow stop me from going to my first day of real school. That morning must have been a milestone for Mother also, since the last of her brood of three would be heading out the door. Freedom.

Lunches sat on the counter: three sets of bologna sandwiches wrapped in wax paper, three stacks of chocolate chip cookies in brand new lunch boxes, ready to be toted off to school. There was lots of scurrying around the house because four people had to share before departing—three kids to school, Mother to work for Eddie Parkins at Sandpoint Cleaners. But on that morning Mother devoted extra time to me. First came the unveiling of the ringlets as she released each section of hair from the mummy rags. Then some touching up here and a little there;

she was proud of her handiwork. Next, the dress. Then one more swipe over the hair. She stood back, beaming with pride over the adorable little girl that she was sending off to the care of Bonner County School District 82.

The boys had gotten themselves ready. As we all grabbed our lunch boxes, once more Mother grabbed a comb. Wetting it, she went through Mike and Kevin's hair, adding the final touches to her trio of angelic offspring. We headed out the door for the bus, and Mother came after us with the camera. We were instructed to line up, tallest to smallest, as she snapped a picture. Then the bus came, and Mother headed back into the house, confident that she, then a single parent, had done her job well. She had sent a darling young lady and two little gentlemen into a world where they would exhibit fine upbringing and be glowing reflections of her admirable maternal efforts.

However, Mother hadn't considered that various factors could tarnish her family's shining images. One of these factors was duration: I had never really been togged out in a dress for any length of time. Trips to church that lasted about an hour, and closely monitored birthday parties did not provide adequate ground training for seven hours of ladylike comportment in school. Mother had forgotten about recess twice daily and the lunch hour. She hadn't thought about the fact that I had never been pinned down in a desk for more than five minutes in my life. She neglected to think of the emotional release I would need after sitting that long. And I don't know how she ever imagined I would suddenly change my recreational habits, which up to that time included galloping several miles a day and practicing dramatic ways of dying in cowboy adventures.

I did not play with dolls when I was a small child. I did not play house. I did not do little girl things and did not even know any little girls, except Pam Doctor who lived across the road from our woods and for some reason didn't spend much time playing with me. I played little boy games because little boys were my role models. My brothers taught me how to make explosive gun sounds with my mouth. We spent hours each day attacking, evading, and dying traumatic deaths in the woods when as adversaries we had subdued one another on our cowboy wars within the bushes and white pine trees. Never once did Mother suit me up in a dress for such combat training.

But my first day with Mrs. Mabel Kinney was a different kind of learning experience. I learned that it wasn't easy to be confined and refined all day, and my mother learned (as soon as she spotted me getting off the bus, miles and miles of ruffles trailing behind me) that she faced an uphill climb in her quest to mold me into anything resembling the word "lady." Mrs. Kinney learned that she had a rascal on her hands.

But I couldn't help it. I left home with the best of intentions, but when recess came I had my band of cowboys organized, and it was awfully hard to race, shoot, and die without picking up a little dirt here and there. I never felt at home with girls who were content to sit around playing with dolls and being pretty. That was not my style and never would be. Instead, in the sixth grade I tried to start a girls' football team. My brothers played on organized teams at school, which meant they needed to practice at home. They needed someone to use as a dummy—guess who? The experience of being repeatedly tackled by Mike and Kevin inspired me to start my own team. One day at recess I gathered my girlfriends together and explained the rules. It was especially gratifying to know that such dainty friends as Lesle Oliver and Laura Delamarter were willing to leave dolls and jump ropes behind to join the ranks of Lincoln School's charter girls' tackle team. Our first male teacher ever, Mr. Scheibe, thought the idea had merit; he even agreed to be our coach.

Our team had only practiced for two days before our principal, Marvel Ekholm, spotted us from a second-floor window, lined up in the three-point stance. Apparently the scene was distressing enough for her to throw out an immediate and effective response. "There'll be no football in dresses!" she barked from her lofty perch. "We'll not have it here!" At first we pretended not to hear her and kept on playing, but she kept on yelling at us—calling me by name. "Marianne, did you hear what I said?" she screamed. "You cannot play football in dresses. Stop it this instant!" Mrs. Ekholm meant business. She'd been our principal since first grade, and we'd all experienced enough of her wrath to put down the football and go back to more ladylike sports like softball.

By the time I finished sixth grade, Mother had seen enough to realize that her efforts to refine me were futile. But she made one last offensive when I entered junior high. The transition seemed like a good opportunity to try some new strategies— bras, lipstick, and girdles. The first bra came one day after I was trying on the cotton slip that had taken me six months to make as a 4-H sewing project. The gurus who dreamed up 4-H believed firmly that if something wasn't done right the first time, you did it over and over and over again until it was acceptable to the critical eye of your fearless leader, an honors graduate of the school of sadism. My cotton slip was a prime example of this philosophy applied. By the time I had ripped out incorrect seams at least twenty times, the finished product looked like it had carefully designed breathing holes. Besides, it was ugly. The undergarment lacked any hint of femininity. It would be an understatement to call it basic. It had no curves, no frills—basically a flour sack with two-inch wide straps.

When I finally brought the slip home, Mother decided I needed to model it for her. As she stood in my bedroom inspecting my handiwork, she became aware that it wasn't harnessing the twin bulges that had burgeoned on my chest. "I'm getting you a bra," she announced decisively. "You'll wear a 38C and you're to wear it all the time from now on." That's how Mother did things. Once the observation was made, the necessary equipment showed up. I was expected to cooperate. Never a lot of discussion. Just do it.

The first few weeks of wearing a bra were traumatic, just like so many other aspects of my adolescent life. I was positive that my bra glowed in the darkness under my shirts and blouses. I was also certain that every time Mike or Kevin walked by they could see the new addition to my ensemble, and that they snickered under their breaths. While other seventh grade girls prayed for anything resembling a bosom, I prayed for mine to cease growing. I even resorted to walking around slightly stoop-shouldered, hoping to hide my twin peaks. It was a year or two before I finally relaxed and decided the need for the breast harness would not go away.

Going into the seventh grade meant more girl surprises, but the one I hated most was Mother's announcement that I must start wearing a girdle and nylons. No more anklets for me, she said; it was time to go down the path to sophistication. It didn't seem to matter to her that I had so far failed to become the demure little mademoiselle she had tried so hard to rear. Like any other mother, she worried about my desirability to the opposite sex if I continued behaving like a hooligan. I don't know why she was so worried. After all, I had received a marriage proposal from Joel Spealman in the second grade. Joel didn't seem to care that I was a ruffian. He dragged me out in the hallway during morning recess one day and insisted that we were getting married.

"I'm not ready yet," I pleaded.

"Let's go get married," he insisted, grabbing my wrist and leading me out the classroom door.

I tried another commonly acceptable ruse. "I'm not old

enough and you don't have a job." I'd been watching a lot of TV.

"That's okay," he continued. "We can get married right now." I don't know what possessed Joel and made him want to marry me at that particular moment, but after a flat-out refusal, he finally let go of my wrist and went on his way. He never renewed the offer.

Actually I had lots of boyfriends during grade school, but the relationships were always a bit shallow. It didn't take much for me to decide if I liked someone. David Harney, who lived near us, was my first victim. Laura Delamarter and I fought for his attention in the first grade. David moved away that summer. Probably a coincidence. Then I fell for Craig Thompson the day he brought his accordion to school. But I was always supposed to like Harmon Cantrell because he went to the Catholic Church and his sister Kathy thought it was a good idea.

Liking a boy was never very serious in grade school. You simply announced to your friends that Mr. X was your current love, wrote his initials on your notebook, and smiled at him. Few of us spent much effort on our grade school romances. But junior high offered whole new dimensions in our lives. There would be dances. There would be hand holding. There would be no more recesses where we could romp carefree around the school grounds. We girls were expected to begin the transition to womanhood. These expectations were Mother's ace-in-the-hole. She knew about hormones and how much young teenage girls want to look nice for young teenage boys. This was her chance to come in for the kill; with biology on her side, she could transform her tomboy daughter into a more acceptable representative of the feminine side of the family.

To begin her new offensive, Mother told me I could wear lipstick. This revelation pleased me. I welcomed the thought of carrying my own personal tube of bright red lipstick in my very first purse. It was definitely grown-up. But Mother also intro-

duced me to a girdle, one of the major garments that distinguished girls from women, since it was time for me to start wearing nylons. By the late 1950s, the breakthrough in hosiery known
as pantyhose may have hit the rest of the world, but in
Sandpoint, Idaho, we were always five years behind the times.
Garter belts and girdles still ruled.

Petite girls needed only a garter belt to hook up hosiery,
but I was not petite. I had been the first student, male or female, to break one hundred pounds in the fifth grade and my
growth spurt had continued. "A girdle will make you slim,"
Mother explained to me. "You'll look ten pounds lighter because
it holds your stomach and firms up your rear end."

So that fall I entered Sandpoint Junior High School with
three items of clothing that represented the severing of ties with
the childhood world of Lincoln School. Although wearing the
bra had become almost a habit, I still folded my arms across my
chest in hopes that nobody would notice it. And on my first day
as a junior high student, I made my own startling observation.
Inspecting the outfits of virtually every other seventh-grade girl
in my six classes, I saw that not one was wearing the same kind
of nylons my mother had bought for me. Shuffling between
classes, sitting on the bleachers during the lunch hour, and
waiting in line after school for the bus to come, I scrutinized
every pair of female legs that walked by, and my panic grew. I
pretended to pay attention and made the expected one-word
responses while my friends discussed cute boys in their math
classes or talked about mean new teachers, but really I was
looking longingly for just one other girl at Sandpoint Junior High
School who was also wearing seamed nylons.

Not one.

On the bus ride home from school, it was difficult to concentrate on conversation while everyone jabbered. My thoughts
turned inside my head instead. I was certainly already an ob-

ject of scorn if anyone had spotted the brown seams that ran crooked trails up the back of my legs. The girdle was bad enough, but wearing something so weird as seamed nylons was more than I could endure.

When I got home, Mother asked how the day had gone. "Oh, it was fine, but do you know what?" I asked. "There are some new kinds of nylons. Everybody has them. They don't have seams. Could you get me some?"

"Your nylons are just fine for school," she replied. "We wore them at Nazareth College. You can wear them to junior high."

"But I'm the only one in the whole school who had seamed nylons today," I protested.

"That's your imagination," she responded. "Besides, maybe you'll start a new trend."

Mother either had forgotten what it felt like to be a self-conscious, clumsy seventh grader who stuck out in a crowd of classmates, or her attendance at Catholic schools, where everyone wore uniforms, had dulled any sensitivity she could have mustered for my embarrassment. The discussion ended. I would continue wearing my seamed stockings to school.

The next day, knowing that my stockings had certainly been the subject of discussion at several dinner conversations, I took every precaution to avoid having anyone see my seams again. I spent a lot of time leaning against lockers, strategically planning my escape through the halls when big crowds of kids pushing their way toward class covered up any clear views of the back of my legs. I walked backward often for the next few days. Somehow even these tactics didn't erase my constant fear of someone catching sight of the seams and yelling out, "Marianne, what kind of ugly stockings are those?"

Finally, after about a week, I came up with a new plan. I would remove my nylons as soon as I got to school. My legs were fat and white, but what the heck? Having people see pale skin did not even come close to having someone comment on my old-fashioned hosiery. Besides, lots of other girls went barelegged.

On my first "ditch the nylons" day, I arrived at school and wasted no time heading for the girls' bathroom on the second floor. Locking myself in a stall and flushing the toilet to distract suspicious souls, I unsnapped the garters, slipped off the stockings, and wadded them up. Social disaster had been averted. Now to hide the hideous hosiery—it wouldn't be cool to dangle from my Peechee folder. I stuffed the ball of nylon in my coat pocket, stuck my coat in my locker, and headed out for what I thought would be a day of relaxed freedom. Before first period, I walked around with my friends feeling as though the weight of the world had been lifted. No longer would I have to plan routes through crowded hallways or spend half the day propped up against walls hiding those wretched seams. I felt like a new woman as I walked into science class with a confident swagger and improved posture. We saluted the flag and listened to morning announcements. Mr. Chronic started his lecture. And then, about two minutes into his talk, I began receiving hints that all was not right with my plan to shed my stockings.

It was 1959, before full-fledged panty girdles, when girdles were still oversized, glorified plastic bands. Mr. Chronic had not yet taught us any physics, so I had no concept of the scientific principles that apply to elastic that has nothing to hold it in place. In fact, I was suddenly incapable of comprehending any science that morning, since my girdle began slowly inching up my thighs in an all-out assault on my waistline.

Pretending to pay close attention to Mr. Chronic, I sat straight up in my desk and tried to grip the seat so the girdle would stay put, maybe even retreat. But It was determined. I could still feel it gradually crawling up the front of my legs. Wiggling my buttocks, I again sat up. This time I lost ground. While I was shifting positions, the girdle took advantage of the temporary loss of pressure and eased a couple of inches upward. Now what?

Still staring straight ahead, I slowly put both hands in my lap and folded them, one on top of the other. I pinched a portion of the girdle with my hidden hand and tried to pull it back down my thigh. But, ready for a long siege, the stubborn elastic refused to move. Switching hands, I tried the other side, all the time aware that all but the most subtle movements could draw the notice of neighboring students who might not be listening closely to Mr. Chronic's lecture. The girdle stood its ground and even advanced, slithering a notch further up my leg.

I looked at the clock. Only ten minutes of first period had passed.

The next forty-five minutes were long, desperate ones. I began to sweat as the girdle maintained its pace upward. I shifted, pinched, and tugged, to no avail. By the end of the hour, I faced another, more vital, challenge—breathing. The bottom portion of the cruel mass of elastic had come to rest on my hips, while the rest hugged my waist. I could barely inhale or exhale; it had squeezed off my lung capacity. Gasping for breath, I imagined the headlines in the *Worldwide Weekly News*, "Girdle Gets Best of North Idaho Sevie."

Never was the expression "saved by the bell" as true as on that miserable morning. When it rang, I exploded from my desk and raced down the crowded hallway toward the lavatory. Within the safety of the stall door, I pulled the garment down as far as it could possibly go without sticking out beneath my skirt. Then I walked ever so slowly to my math class on the second floor of the junior high annex, trying not to disturb my girdle and hoping it would stay put this hour. Once in the room, I sat down carefully, exerting maximum pressure on the back of my knees to nail the thing down. Mr. Loman joked around for a minute and then began his lecture.

Now, one thing I hadn't thought of during my race to the lavatory was why people normally use that facility. My oversight became more and more apparent as Mr. Loman started explaining fractions. My bladder had not been given any relief since I left home at 7:30, and wouldn't be able to get any for at least another hour. Obviously, during the first week of seventh grade in a brand new school, I couldn't draw attention to myself by asking to go to the bathroom during class. I had a real battle on my hands, fending off two offensives—one enemy within that wanted to blow up and another outside that wanted to scale the mountain.

"Why did I do this?" I thought to myself. "I shoulda just left the nylons on. Why do I have to be so weird?" Having a dialogue with myself during class was not helpful. Anytime I took my mind off the girdle It took advantage of me and wormed its way up my legs. My bladder pulsated, constantly reminding me that it wanted its contents out. The more miserable it made me, the more I shifted around in my seat. Eventually the girdle took charge. With relative ease, it found its way back up to my waistline. Surrendering on that front, I could concentrate on squeezing my legs together to avoid any outburst from my bladder. But a second defeat seemed certain.

The longest hour of my life finally ended. Again I shot out of my desk and ran out the math class door in a flurry, oblivious to anyone blocking my pathway to relief. Throwing open the bathroom door and banging into the stall, I bent down, ripped off the girdle, and opened the bladder gates. Once the flood had subsided, I made another undergarment decision. "Never again," I thought. "The girdle's gotta go, too." I stuffed it in my purse and ran to third period reading class. The rest of the school day passed smoothly, but the morning had produced enough stress to last me for the rest of my junior high career.

When the final bell rang I headed to the lavatory for one

last visit—to get fully dressed for the bus ride home. Mother would be horrified if she ever had any inkling I had altered the ensemble she had approved as I walked out the door that morning. She had given me plenty of reason to believe that debating the hosiery/girdle issue was a lost cause. Her word stood, and I knew better than to question it. The clandestine approach was the only way to keep us both happy.

So I started a new routine the next day and followed it regularly. Leave the house with approved outfit. Keep the backs of my legs hidden or in perpetual motion while encountering groups of peers. Enter the school. Before dumping everything at my locker, go to the lavatory. Pull off the girdle and nylons, roll them up in a ball, and stuff them in my coat pocket. Make the locker deposit, and be off down the hallway. When the school day ends, reverse the routine. Hide among the crowd while waiting for the bus. Go home to a satisfied, unsuspecting mother. I adhered to this routine for the next three years. Mother never questioned why my nylons stayed in such good condition, even though she must have thought it strange that a clumsy oaf like me could keep something so delicate unsullied for so long.

Along with high school came a softening of Mother's insistence that seamed nylons were the only way to go; I was finally allowed to wear the seamless variety. And since panty girdles had appeared on the scene, it was a whole new world. I thought I could leave my years of lingerie misery behind. But during my sophomore year in Mrs. Houghton's Honors English class there came an embarrassing revelation.

My classmates and I had each drawn the name of another who would serve as the subject of an introduction speech. Joanne Buhr, my eighth-grade locker partner, drew my name. I picked hers. During our year as locker mates, neither of us had any clue of how to keep a locker neat, but I always thought Joanne was a bigger slob that I. I also thought this information would be fun to share with our English class.

My speech came first. Of course, I told the class all the good stuff about Joanne. She was pretty. Her intellect was impressive—in fact, she later helped me pass chemistry. We enjoyed debating about which was the better church, Lutheran or Catholic. I had gone to slumber parties at her house.

Being a pretty fair public speaker, I knew how to work an audience. The class was mesmerized as I strategically inserted pregnant pauses between tidbits of information. And as any good orator would do, I saved the best for last. "Oh, yes, one more thing . . . she's a slob as a locker partner," I proclaimed. "She keeps moldy oranges and old lunches stuffed among her books." The audience chuckled. "She didn't clean her part of the locker for the whole year," I added. "In fact, it started to smell toward the end."

Everybody devoured this information with great glee. The class was laughing and so was I. I had stolen the show. Even Joanne feigned amusement, her half-smile hiding any resentment she might have felt at the moment. I sat down, satisfied that I'd earned my A.

But when Joanne's turn to speak came the next day, she followed my strategy and worked up toward the knockout punch. "Marianne lives on a farm and she likes horses. She goes to the Catholic church, which is not her fault. She also has two little sisters and two big brothers." She continued to list the everyday, boring details that make up most teenagers' lives. Finally, staring me straight in the face, she let loose with the big one.

"Marianne had one odd habit," she began. I thought maybe she was going to tell how I always ate the crust off Laura Delamarter's tuna fish sandwiches at lunch time. I had forgotten that she had long been privy to the privates I kept stashed in our locker. She was armed for a direct hit. "She stuffs female unmentionables in her coat pocket," Joanne disclosed. An explosion of giggles and shrieks filled the room and filtered out into the hallway. All eyes shot my way as the snickers and snorts continued interminably. That was all Joanne had to say. Her blue eyes gleaming, she dealt me a satisfied look and sat down.

Her revelation was the talk of the afternoon classes. Back in those days, "unmentionables" covered a broad range. Kids could think of anything—and no doubt did. I could say nothing. Joanne's retaliation was complete, and I had had it coming.

By my junior year, Mother's dream of my ever becoming a lady had slowly vanished. She relaxed in the knowledge that there was no point in pursuing the impossible. And there were two good new reasons for her attitude—my younger sisters. Maybe I was a failed candidate for the femininity brigade, but now she had Barbara and Laurie to work on. She'd have greater luck with the Batch Two girls.

Poor Mother.

Barbara and Laurie gained fame, not for their fashion flair, but for leading the Lincoln School softball batting squad.

The NUTS and BOLTS of JUNIOR HIGH CHOIR

Dona Meehan still speaks to me. I don't know why.

More than thirty years ago, she attempted to teach me to sing. Since those days in the seventh grade at Sandpoint Junior High School, my cacophonous second soprano voice has caused many a head to swivel in amazement. Numerous small children have listened to me belt out "Amazing Grace" at Sunday Mass only to tug away at their mom's coat, coaxing her to gawk along with them at the funny sounding lady. When I warble some of my favorites like "Climb Every Mountain" and "Somewhere over the Rainbow," I know deep down that suffering ears yearn to climb somewhere out there far, far away.

climb somewhere out there far, far away.

Mrs. Meehan's failure to teach me to carry a tune is not the only sour note she suffered because of me. Besides enduring my total lack of talent for one full school year, this affable music teacher from Wisconsin foiled a plot my chums and I crafted with our own hands—and knees. Had Mrs. Meehan not caught us in the act, our plans might have led to our permanent public banishment and her permanent abandonment of the teaching profession.

When I first laid eyes on Mrs. Meehan, I was a fifth grader sitting in a classroom desk at Lincoln School. One day the school principal, Mrs. Ekholm, opened the door connecting the fifth and sixth grade rooms. She introduced Mrs. Meehan as the new music teacher for the school district. Having listened to Mrs. Ekholm pound on the piano and her less than melodious voice for five years, our class's appreciation of music and the people who created it was not exactly enthusiastic. However, when Mrs. Meehan stood in the doorway between those two classrooms transfixing us with a rich, powerful soprano solo to "Bless This House," I knew God had to be smiling on her. If I said enough "Hail Marys," maybe He'd smile on me too, and maybe someday I could sing just like Mrs. Meehan.

Two years later, I sat in Mrs. Meehan's beginning choir class, which met sixth period in the three-hundred-seat auditorium on the third floor of Sandpoint Junior High School. My mother, blunt as ever, had been unable to stifle her amusement when she saw "choir" listed on my seventh grade schedule. "You'll never be able to sing," she assured me. "You're tone deaf." Mother always intimidated me with her tactless appraisals of my talents. But I defied her by enrolling in choir, and was bound and determined to prove her wrong.

One of my first breaks came when Mrs. Meehan informed us that we would have to sing and talk loudly and clearly, for she was deaf in one ear. That seemed wonderful to me—a tone deaf singer with a deaf instructor. I had it made. As the first few weeks passed, Mrs. Meehan, aided by a cupped hand over her ear, sat at the piano and listened to us belt out our scales. I didn't really mind being classified a second soprano until I learned that such designation required me to sing harmony. This was a huge disappointment, as I preferred singing the melody. The situation also marked one up for Mother, since anytime anyone harmonized in my ear, whatever I happened to be singing would trail off into an unrecognizable and unpleasant alien tune. This still happens today; it has continued to be one of my mother's most effective means of demoralizing me musically. She delights in baiting me by starting the melody of some old familiar favorite like "Silent Night." Unable to resist the temptation, I chime in. For approximately ten notes, she continues the melody, then, as my confidence builds, her deep alto voice sneaks into harmony. Once again, I'm a goner.

In seventh grade choir, however, I had some points in my favor. I sat in the middle of fifteen other second sopranos who sang loud enough to drown out the melody and whatever notes the altos had to sing. Also, Mrs. Meehan often had two of us sing together rather than listening to each of us individually, and whoever happened to be my partner usually carried the notes well enough to carry me, too. It worked well enough that Mrs. Meehan may never have really known what Mother knew about my singing.

We rehearsed for concerts and learned names like Dvorak, Rogers and Hammerstein, and Stephen Foster. "Dry Bones" and "Bali Hai" became familiar to our tongues and ears.

We also learned how to faint. The subject came up one day when Mrs. Meehan told us how to stand on choral risers without locking our knees. If we locked them, we might keel over right in the middle of our concert and be humiliated for life.

While talking about accidental faintings, Mrs. Meehan must have had a weak moment; she actually gave us instructions on how to faint on purpose. The instructions were so simple we didn't even need to write them down. "Get down on your haunches," she explained. "Take ten deep breaths, then jump up and blow really hard on your thumb."

Within two days at least four of us had become statistics. We *did* try it at home. Some fainted in front of friends but, being fairly independent, I chose to solo. My only audience was my one-month-old sister Barbara. Barbara eventually led her class as valedictorian but she was not an infant prodigy; she watched me from her bassinet, but couldn't tattle. I distinctly recall going through the crouch-and-breathe routine. But I don't remember falling on the floor. I do remember Mother's stern voice coming from the living room.

"Marianne, what was that crash?" she yelled.

Picking myself up and feeling a painful knot where my head had collided with the floor, I managed to stifle my groans long enough to answer, "Oh, I just dropped my books on the floor."

Since Mother was fairly glued to the latest Hughes family problems on *As the World Turns*, she bought the lie and didn't question further. I spent the rest of the afternoon nursing my wound and vowing that I would never make myself faint again. But I certainly had a good skill to teach to friends at future slumber parties.

During that first year of junior high choir we put on three concerts—one in the fall, one at Christmas, and another in the spring. After each performance Mrs. Meehan took a break from trying to teach the thirty of us to sing as a group. For two or three weeks we were to bring our books and use choir hour as a study hall while she gave individual vocal tests. To ensure good behavior, she separated us throughout the auditorium. We each sat in our own row with two or three empty rows between us. In our all-girl group, no one would have stood out above the others in a talking contest. We were all skilled in that department; in fact, our talking talent far exceeded our singing ability. Mrs. Meehan was smart to take the preventive measure of special seating. Her plan failed to combat all of our potential impishness, however. She had perceived that she had a troupe of incurable motor mouths, but fell short in evaluating our other dimensions. We were an inspired group, ready and able to try anything to add a little pizzazz to each day.

That year, as we converged on junior high from Farmin, Washington, Sagle, and Lincoln Elementary schools, we got to know one another quickly. Talented class leaders like Judy Hagadone soon emerged from the pack, especially in Mrs. Morris's literature class. While Eddie Bangeman sat in the corner informing Mrs. Morris that he had just hit six hundred words per minute on the most recent reading test, Judy entertained the rest of us with her muscle control trick. Staring expressionlessly at an admiring audience, she would inconspicuously manipulate the muscles around her skull, thereby moving her ears up and down at least an inch each direction. Judy's was a talent I attempted to learn for years, but never quite mastered. Judy also served as the gang leader of the choir class crime. Of the girls involved, I was the last to join the subversive ring that cracked Mrs. Meehan's foolproof classroom management plan, inciting her to wrath unlike anything I'd ever seen before or since.

It all started about a week into our post-Christmas-concert seating arrangement. Surveying my colleagues midway through class one day, I noticed that some of them were missing. This seemed odd because they had come into the room when class started and I couldn't recall any of them asking to leave. I didn't think too much about it the first day, but the next, after some more vigilant observation, I knew something was awry.

Peering around the great hall shortly after roll call, I searched for Judy, JoAnn Rogers, and Marilynn McKenney. No sign of any of them. "Hmm!" I thought. "Looks pretty interesting." It became more intriguing when, as the bell rang, the three showed up in the crowd heading out the door.

Never one to miss out on the fun, I followed them down the hall. At first, despite my skilled interrogation, they were unwilling to divulge their clandestine activities. Finally they relented and told me that each day after roll call a secret signal cued them to disappear and begin their work.

Some work!!!

Slowly, subtly, each girl removed herself from her chair and crouched down on her hands and knees, fully out of sight, to methodically remove screws, nuts, and bolts from the auditorium chairs. The grand plan was to dismantle them all. As a first step, the steering committee had no greater goal than getting the hardware and not getting caught.

Pretty neat, I thought. "Hey, can I help you?" I begged.

Judy and her chums didn't have much choice, because they knew me well enough to know I never passed an opportunity for a good prank. If they said no, they knew I'd find a way to participate anyway.

I couldn't wait. The intrigue had far more appeal than sitting still for an hour reading about pyramids in my social studies book. The next day I went to class brimming over with excitement about my initiation into Judy's exclusive group of choir thugs. After all, when you came from "Stinkin' Lincoln," you had an image to overcome among the downtown elementary school grads. We were sure they looked upon us as lowlifes because the kids who attended Lincoln weren't exactly trust-fund babies. Being accepted into Judy's inner circle represented an important milestone in my rise to the top of the junior high pantheon.

When class started, we went to our assigned seats as usual. Mrs. Meehan took roll then quickly involved herself in a vocal testing project on the stage. Throughout the enormous room, choir members ostensibly started their studies. However, a few of us put books aside and waited for the opportunity to duck out of sight. One by one, members of Judy's crew disappeared from view. My time came. Putting all my books on the seat next to me, I slid forward, turned my knees to the left, and cautiously lowered myself to the floor. Fortunately, the gray wooden seats did not flip up like those in more modern auditoriums, so I didn't have to worry about that noise, but the combination of my knees and the shiny hardwood floor presented a different dilemma. That floor squeaked with the slightest hint of movement. I had to be careful to avoid attracting Mrs. Meehan's attention.

Once on all fours, I squeezed down to peek underneath the seats for the other members of the crew. That proved more dangerous than a squeaky floor. Throughout my life, I've suffered from a severe lack of restraint. It doesn't take much to humor me, so the sight of one of my cohorts scrunched down on the auditorium floor several rows away seemed pretty funny. I needed to giggle, but I also knew at that moment it was critical to stifle all emotional outbursts. The challenge was almost too much, but I managed to subdue my impulses. I had screws to steal.

Slowly, carefully, I slid forward, one knee at a time, to a selected seat, all the while restraining my glee at being a select member of the conspiracy. Our specific task was to remove the screws that fastened the upraised seats to the main base. Located on the bottom side of the chairs, the bolts and screws apparently had not been tightened since the ornate auditorium was first built in the late 1920s, so it was fairly easy to grab hold of the nuts and loosen them by hand.

I approached my first seat. Grabbing the nut, I twirled it

around with ease, and in no time had myself a bolt, some washers, and the nut. The ecstasy was too much; I had to display my
booty to another conspirator. While lowering my body to signal
Judy, I suddenly sensed a disturbing presence. It was not a good
feeling. A looming, ominous magnet pulled my head upward,
and my eyes focused on a most horrendous sight. Over me stood
Mrs. Meehan, glaring with hideous ire. Her body was rigid as
she extended her hand.

"Give it here!" she intoned.

Sweat instantly sprang from my brow as a jolt of panic
electrified my body. I hunkered there, frozen like a toppled Greek
statue, all muscles refusing to cooperate. I weighed my options.
This was pre-*Star Trek*, so having Scotty beam me up wasn't in
the cards. Pray for invisibility? Head for home? I thought about
leaping up, running out, and never coming back, but with the
auditorium maze, the two flights of stairs, and those heavy exit
doors, I knew I'd probably permanently maim myself in my
escape.

I finally resorted to the only logical (though it seemed dumb
at the time) choice left. Handing the bolt, nut, and washers to
Mrs. Meehan, I slowly rose from the floor, returned to my seat
and sat down. Quietly, methodically, Mrs. Meehan swept the
auditorium until the remaining conspirators were revealed.
Meanwhile, all the innocent do-gooders in the choir delighted in
our capture, assuming holier-than-thou stares and giggling
fiendishly. With incriminating hardware in hand, Mrs. Meehan
dismissed class. We criminals, however, were ordered to stay.

We later discovered that some important information had
failed to reach our ears that day. During an earlier gathering in
the auditorium, Jay Miller, an eighth grader, had sat down in
one of the tampered seats only to have it crash to the floor. The
band director, Lee Robinson, inspected the scene and discovered that no nuts and bolts could be found anywhere near the

chair. Suspicious, he surveyed other seats and observed that many were missing vital parts of their anatomy. Word of his discovery spread to selected ears, but we conspirators had no idea we were in for a sting operation on the very day I joined the ring. As part of the faculty police squad that day, Mrs. Meehan was to nab and nark.

My memories of the events immediately following our capture remain a fog; actually, I think my mind ceased all active functions. Much like a robot's, my body mechanically responded to all outside stimuli. The only really clear vision came the next day as we sat at attention while Mrs. Meehan displayed the mountain of screws, nuts, and bolts on top of the piano. I'd estimate that at least 250 pieces of metal made up that pile. She glared at us. We sat motionless and silent as she carefully crafted her remarks. "I'm disappointed with you," she said. "How can I ever trust you again? Don't you know how dangerous that could have been? I've never seen anything like it. . . ."

Her words trailed on. We failed to show much emotion. Everyone simply stared back, numb with the knowledge that we were at her mercy. Then she prepared us for the upcoming visitor, a force none of us welcomed that day.

One of the double doors opened. A chorus of eyes darted to the right as the General George S. Patton of Sandpoint Junior High School marched into the room. A sixty-year-old World War II veteran who had entered the teaching profession only a few years before, Principal Charlie Stidwell had already become a Sandpoint legend by the time we entered junior high. A tough but caring disciplinarian who ran a tight ship, Mr. Stidwell commanded respect wherever he went—whether it was standing at the bottom of the stairway inspecting boys' pants for missing belts or sitting in his office dishing out firm, fair, and memorable punishment for students who had gone astray. On that day, Charlie (as many of us fondly referred to him) had rigorous duty ahead of him as Mrs. Meehan summarized the situation. "Mr. Stidwell and I have discussed this problem," she announced, "and he has something to say to you."

We knew he'd have plenty to say.

As he began to speak, Charlie maintained a stance that must have been rehearsed many times before a full-length mirror. With hands firmly fisted on his hips, he emphatically glowered down at us, his glare somehow meeting each set of eyes head-on. Obvious disgust manifested itself in his face, crimson with anger, his jaw on both sides pulsating like that of an overly agitated bullfrog. The entire choir had to withstand the tonguelashing that followed. Charlie had carefully orchestrated his speech to purge guilt from every ounce of our twelve-year-old bodies. He preached. He humiliated. He embarrassed. He threatened. He chastised. Shakespeare could have improved on Marc Antony's famous funeral oration for Caesar if he'd been there to listen and watch Charlie that day.

Fifteen minutes later he left the room, satisfied he had inflicted fear that would last for decades. The impact of his words left us drained. Charlie's tactic had been to strip us of all dignity and of any hope that we might ever become anything in life. "You've dishonored yourselves, your parents, and this school," he told us. "Anyone committing this kind of vandalism doesn't deserve to be accepted into Honor Society."

"No-o-o-o!" I silently responded within my paralyzed frame. When Charlie uttered those words, my heart skipped at least seventeen beats. Mother expected me to be in Honor Society. Until that day, I'd been a shoo-in. My As and Bs were more than adequate to meet the requirements. Charlie's words meant big trouble on the home front. My mind went into overdrive, analyzing just how I'd get out of this fix. Mother must never find out that I'd allowed myself to get involved with the other choir criminals, let alone that I'd actually sought out the association.

It would make no difference to her that I was just a new recruit to the screw crew. She always made the same retort.

"I don't care what anyone else has done," she'd say. "I just care about you."

So I was relieved when Charlie dangled a carrot—even one that offered no real guarantees, only a faint ray of hope that there was a way to redeem ourselves. "You might be able to do something to make up for this," he suggested. "If you do some good deed that benefits the school and if you stay out of trouble in every single class for the rest of the school year."

I would do it. I would perform a task which would count as a good deed for the school, thereby getting myself off the hook with Mrs. Meehan and Charlie. In addition, I would earn a C in one of my classes, giving myself another excuse for not making the honor roll and putting me out of contention for Honor Society. Grades were important in our household, but they didn't rank as high as decency, honor, and good citizenship. Besides, I could always get into Honor Society the next semester.

When Mrs. Meehan recorded our good deeds pledges, the other guilty students drew prime jobs such as rearranging the trophy case on the second floor. My duty was to dust the piano. I would have preferred to perform my task at that very moment, to erase the black guilt that now shackled my soul, and, of course, to erase the paralyzing fear of my parents ever finding out its source, but no class time was allowed. We had to find our own time to do our tasks.

I had to wait until the next day to do mine. Before leaving for school that morning I sneaked a dust rag from the utility drawer in the kitchen and stuffed it between my books. At school, I checked the auditorium doors frequently in between morning classes, hoping for a chance to scurry in and do the dusting while no one was looking. At noontime, I was finally able to perform my penance—too hastily, however. While priming us for scale warm-ups, Mrs. Meehan stopped for an instant and inspected the piano top. Rubbing her fingers over the surface, she surveyed them and then looked directly at me.

"Did you really dust this?" she inquired.

Twenty-nine pairs of eyes focused on me as I slid lower in my seat. "Yeah," I responded, in a voice just above a whisper.

Her look of skepticism indicated that my effort hadn't completely satisfied her. However, nothing more was said about the piano dusting job, the original crime, or our prospects regarding Honor Society. Mrs. Meehan and the choir members moved on with an unspoken agreement to put the whole embarrassing experience behind us. As the months wore on, I could not bring myself to work for a C in any class. Banking on the odds that good behavior and time would erase memories of my black-hearted deed, I went on about the business of being an awkward seventh grader with good grades.

My choir career ended that year—not because of the nuts and bolts incident, and not because of Mother's continual humiliating appraisals of my singing, but because of an experience at the spring choral contests in Coeur d'Alene. The seventh and eighth grade choirs combined forces for that event, so no longer did I sing next to the forgiving ears of friends. Instead my notes dribbled over toward Gracie Nordgaarden, who stood to my left as we began the songs for our contest. She had apparently never heard anything quite like it. When we had completed the first number, she turned to me and asked, "Are you singing the same song as the rest of us?" During the remaining numbers, not a sound came from my throat. I just went through the motions, silently mouthing the words. Gracie had unwittingly convinced me of something Mother had been trying to tell me for years. I had no singing talent.

The following summer a letter arrived in the mail. It was an invitation to join National Junior Honor Society. Mother never knew that I once viewed that honor as a mixed blessing.

Several years later, I returned to Sandpoint to teach English at Sandpoint High School. One of my colleagues was none other than Dona Meehan, who still cupped her hand to hear young girls' voices. She has since retired and also has forgiven me. Judy Hagadone still lives in Sandpoint, too. She has consented to give me lessons on how to make my ears go up and down, but we've agreed put off our practice until we're tenants at the Odd Fellows Senior Citizens' Plaza.

KIDS, DOGS, and COWS, etc.

The note read, "It's okay to send your dogs to work, but from now on send them with a lunch and a hard hat."

We didn't have any extra hard hats, so we decided they would no longer show up for the night shift at the local lumber mill.

Bogey and Julie are our dogs' proper names, though they've had several others. "Damn dogs" ranks among the top choices. This epithet has been uttered a time or two at 2:30 in the morning when the phone has rung, and the voice at the other end has announced, "Your dogs are here."

Much like those eyes in the country western hit, our brother-and-sister English setters have been known for wandering. I call them "Gone Dogs" because that's what these mutts manage

Virginia O. Tibbs '80

to be much of the time—gone from our home. They have become notorious throughout Sandpoint, as numerous residents have spotted them sniffing pavement, dirt, grass, gravel, and other doggie deposits anywhere from the local Serv-a-burger to the Panida Theater. One time they even ended up at the home of the White Elephant proprietor forty-five miles away in Coeur d'Alene. It seems they'd jumped in the back of his pickup while he was having a cup of coffee at the local cafe one evening. The dogs made themselves at home and were in deep-snooze as he pulled away and headed for the road.

Our dogs are truly man's best friends. In fact, they're best friends to anyone who happens to meet up with them on their haunts about the countryside. Just about everyone who gets to know the two tramps has an interesting story to relate and a certain reluctance for us to reclaim them because "they're such nice dogs." These temporary hosts have never kept our pets long enough to know their true personalities. They are canine Jekyll-and-Hydes. Bogey and Julie can be wonderful pets to the kids, great companions for a jog or hike in the mountains, and loyal friends whose loving expressions can melt the heart of any callous soul. But these two chameleons have sinned enough to keep a priest in a quandary over proper penance. Their sin: abandonment. These rascals can disappear into thin air and relocate five miles away before you can blink your eye. In doing so, they have embarrassed us beyond belief.

One of their jaunts caused us to be the object of a scathing commentary in the "Pet Corner" column of the Sandpoint Daily Bee. On that particular escape, the two had lost their name tags sometime before they met up with a woman named Wynona while lounging at entrance to the Bonner Mall. Wynona took them home, then turned them over to the local animal protection unit, which took them to the local veterinary hospital. By this time enough people had seen the two that they were eventually identified as ours.

The lady in charge of the animal protection unit was horrified that people would allow their dogs to run at large without identification, so she wrote about us in her newspaper column. By the time she had raked certain dog owners over the coals, *we* needed no identification. Our dogs had been to enough people's houses that her description of two English setters with blue collars struck a familiar note in the minds of half the town.

Bogey and Julie especially liked to visit the local lumber mill, where they begged for handouts from the graveyard crew in the lunch room. Two nights in a row we received calls, long after midnight, to come and pick them up. It was on the morning following Bill's second middle-of-the-night trip to the mill that we found the note about dogs and hardhats attached to Julie's collar. It was the last straw. Since that time we have kept one dog tied up at all times, and they both stay home— they believe in teamwork.

I've known nutty animals ever since my early years at the North Boyer farm. One of these pets was another English setter named Hi-Tone Lady Peg (nicknamed Peggy) who came west on the train with Mother in 1945. As far back as I can remember, Peggy was firmly established as head dog at our place. She found life on the North Boyer farm to her liking. Kids and barnyard puddles kept her busy. Peggy had also acquired an in-house nickname: Lickerlap.

Lickerlap joined us at mealtime around the yellow kitchen table, devotedly watching every molecule of food on its journey from serving bowl to plate to mouth. Unfortunately, my bites didn't always follow the planned itinerary. About three of every four took side trips—from serving bowl to plate to lap. A bite of steak tumbled into the unplanned depository, initiating a contest between my fumbling fingers and Lickerlap's tongue. Score one for the dog and zero for me, nine times out of ten. All that remained in my lap was a healthy deposit of slimy froth, one of her best weapons in the bite battle. It diminished my interest in retrieving lost morsels that dribbled to my upper thighs.

Lickerlap made me look ridiculous at the dinner table, but she had her moments in the barnyard. I often spent my mornings sitting in the sun at the granary, scribbling away in the dirt with a twig. Those moments of tranquility were interrupted when Peggy ambled through and discovered a large dog looking back at her from the huge, rust-colored mud puddle just inside the barnyard gate. Peggy never figured out that she was actually talking to herself as she chastised the dog in the puddle. She waged daily wars with the mirror image. The more severely she growled and barked at the animal, the nastier its retaliation. She lunged at it. It lunged back. She growled. It growled. She shook her head and cocked it to one side. The puddle dog did the same. Peggy's incessant vocal abuse drove me crazy. I tried to explain to her that she was wasting her barks, but she ignored my counseling. Her only reaction was to steal more food from my lap at lunch time during her breaks from the seemingly endless battle with her barnyard nemesis. The war ended only when the barnyard dried up and the dog disappeared until the next big rainstorm.

Along with Peggy, we had an Irish setter named Kit and a springer spaniel named Laddie. Peggy and Laddie hit it off and produced a litter of puppies. We gave them all away except one named Duffy. You couldn't tell from Duffy's looks that a few chromosomes were missing. He was a beautiful black and white dog with a big smile and a perpetual wag to his tail. We often wondered what Duffy was thinking about because he seemed to be forever in deep thoughts—well, happy thoughts, anyway. His bliss was temporarily marred one day as we watched him wag and smile his way underneath our electric fence. When his tail connected with the wire, Duffy let out a yipe loud enough for neighbors to hear. He then composed himself, wandered on across the field, and blissfully returned via the same route, wagging away and hitting the wire again. It took Duffy time to learn things. Watching him torture himself, we knew he definitely had a learning disability.

This was proven the day Harold took us all down to Sand Creek on the back of his Chevy flatbed. Kids and dogs were having a nice time until we passed by a neighbor's house where a big, bad wolf lived. This loud-mouthed dog barked out a warning to all other four-legged creatures who dared pass. It was more than Duffy could take. He was insulted, so he flung a few insults toward the overzealous watchdog, only to be outbarked. That really incensed him.

"WOOF—WOOF—WOOOF—WOOOF—WOOOOF—EEEE — YYYIIIPPPPEEEE — YYYYIIIPPPEEEE — YIPE—YIPE—yipe." Duffy had gotten so involved in his canine tongue-lashing that he forgot everything else. He forgot that he was on a moving truck. He forgot that it was going forty-five miles per hour, and he forgot just how bad it feels to hit nose first in the gravel after walking off the back end of a truck.

As Duffy hit the road, a chorus of kids yelled, "Stop!!!!" Harold brought the flatbed to rest. Immediately we all jumped off and scurried down the road to survey the damage. Lying in a heap in the middle of the road, Duffy whined and moaned with pain. The offending guard dog smiled, licked his chops, and lay down in his yard, content that once more he had defended the premises. Duffy recovered from his scrapes, but he never got any smarter.

Duffy was not the only one of our animals who believed in "No pain, no gain." Shortly after moving to the farm in 1950, Mother purchased a milk cow from Guy Hesselgesser, an old cowboy who kept horses and cows in town. Bossy was a dehorned Guernsey. Her large belly and scrawny legs were covered with slick, solid brown hide. Bossy walked the woods and barnyard on hooves that could always use a good trim. Her warm, loving eyes and flesh-colored muzzle made her a hit with all humans. She liked people. Bossy had the biggest teats I've ever seen on a milk cow. They looked like four oversized German sausages dangling from her udder, and when she walked they flopped from side to side. She liked to wander the neighborhood. A barbed wire fence meant nothing to her, and her teats took a slashing as the barbs punctured them while she crawled through, looking for greener pastures. Mother finally put a yoke around Bossy's neck to discourage her from leaving home.

When they were not being treated for wire cuts, Bossy's handles made it easy for novice milkers to squeeze out lots of rich milk and thick cream twice daily. When Bossy eventually passed on, we knew there'd never be an udder quite like hers. Bossy provided enough nutrition for our family and each year's baby calf, which eventually became part of the provisions stored in each year's locker box.

Mother also tried raising rabbits for the dinner table. She soon found that the meat was not a favorite with the family. It seems that Mike had just finished reading about Peter Rabbit when he happened upon my father butchering the family bunnies. He passed the word to the rest of us. That night's rabbit stew went over as poorly as the dried up, leather-tough antelope Mother once tried to sneak into the pot. She failed to get away with either. Bunnies and antelope never roamed across our plates again.

Mike was opinionated when it came to certain animals—for instance, the pony Mother bought him for his seventh birthday. When Pat Gooby delivered Tony, the little horse was beautifully groomed and adorned with a large red bow around his girth. We all stood and admired him; I felt a little jealous and wondered when my very own horse would be coming. Tony was a real hit with the family until the day Mike decided to ride him without any supervision and without a saddle or bridle. The only gear he had to control the pony was a halter and lead rope. He also had nothing to grab on to because Tony's mane had been roached. When Mike got on, Tony took off at a dead run across the field filled with stumps. In no time, my big brother fell off and broke his arm. From that day forth, Mike never had the desire to ride Tony again. He also took up the new view that all horses were "monsters."

Our menagerie continued to grow over the years. We spent lots of time chasing down horses that had been down in the back pasture eating contentedly when suddenly a gong inside their heads alerted them that some kid had left the barnyard gate open. Within seconds eight horses pranced arrogantly down Boyer with tails and noses in the air. Seconds later, Harold headed for the barn after a halter and grain bucket, chiding the irresponsible kids. "How many times have I told you to Shut The Gate?" he muttered as the rest of us hot-footed it outside to help bring back the herd.

One time we had to—oops—I'd like to continue talking about kids, dogs, and cows. But I just looked up to see my huge horse Rambo staring back at me through the living room window, with a six-foot cornstalk in his mouth, hinting that he'd like to come in and watch TV.

THEY TOOK *the* CAKE

Lucille Hudon and Eleanor Delamarter supervised some of the most miserable moments of my life. They were my first 4-H leaders, and I never really knew whether to thank or smack them. I'm sure there were times they would gladly have done the latter to me.

Mother had high hopes when she enrolled me in the Mountain View ABC 4-H Club in 1957. I had just finished a rather successful fourth-grade stint with Mrs. Alberta Sutliff, but it was time to start broadening my domestic skills. I had brought home information about Girl Scouts, but Mother was not a fan of Scouting. Her prejudice was reinforced when Kevin brought home his brand new sleeping bag from a week-long stay at the Boy Scout camp on Lake Coeur d'Alene. She wouldn't allow it near the house. It stunk of mildew inside and out, and was coated with globs of grimy mud. It was eventually hauled to the dump. Mother preferred 4-H. Harold already led a 4-H livestock club and the home ec club wouldn't require trips into some den mother's house in town. The leadership was located right in our neighborhood, within walking distance of my house. Besides, she rather liked the lofty 4-H motto that promised to "Make the Best Better."

I wasn't too keen on enrolling in home ec club, especially since both of my brothers got to join Harold's livestock group. For some masochistic reason I actually wanted to follow in the footsteps of those unmerciful souls who constantly tormented me, but Mother reminded me that I was a girl and that I needed to do what other girls my age did. "You're going to take cooking and arts and crafts to start out," she announced as we drove to Mrs. Hudon's house.

"I want to take a cow," I pleaded.

"If you do a good job this first year, maybe you can take beef next year," she promised as she dropped me off at the Hudons and went on her way.

Once inside, I felt better when I saw some of my classmates and other girls who rode the same bus I did. Everybody milled around for a while, until we were all called to attention and told to stand and look at a pair of flags sitting on the table. Genevieve, Mrs. Hudon's daughter, led the group in both the "Pledge of Allegiance" and the "4-H Pledge." Those of us who were new stood dumbfounded, watching hands and fingers flying from chest to head to chest to opera pose to military attention. It was quite a sight for anyone who didn't have a clue what all the hand jive meant.

At that first meeting the leaders explained the purpose of 4-H, then outlined their expectations. "You'll have to finish your projects. You must give a demonstration. And you must attend all meetings," Mrs. Hudon told us. "You must also fill out this record book. And there will be dues. We follow parliamentary procedure at our meetings."

This information overloaded my ten-year-old mind. "What's so great about this stuff?" I thought. "All it is is work." My negative impression of this new addition to my schedule got deeper as the meeting wore on. I knew I would hate every minute of 4-H . . . until Mrs. Hudon and Genevieve left the room temporarily and returned with a beautiful sight. "Refreshments!" they announced.

Instantly the 4-H ratings soared. "Hmm," I thought, "Maybe this isn't so bad." The platter filled with fresh-baked chocolate chip cookies and the tray lined with cups of cherry Kool-Aid punch brought a smile to my face and renewed my interest in being there. "When's the next meeting?" I asked, grabbing four cookies and a cup of juice. I gathered up my materials, and headed for the door. Mothers had arrived and were talking to Mrs. Hudon about events to come. There were still cookies left on the platter. No one was looking, so I slunk by, gathered up another handful, and left.

"How did it go?" Mother asked as I got into the car, still chomping away on my booty.

"It's great," I said. "They serve refreshments."

Thereafter Mother had no problem getting me to the meetings, since I knew a reward waited each time. I could put up with all that parliamentary stuff, the pledge, and working on projects. But I didn't exactly like any of it.

That first year we made funny-looking baskets in arts and crafts and learned some stuff about cooking. However, Mother doubted just how much knowledge was being imparted at the meetings the day I told her I was ready to make vanilla pudding from scratch. My Cooking I manual open to the recipe, I assured her that I knew perfectly well what I was doing. Convinced by my confidence, she headed for the barn to brush the horses.

It was great to have the kitchen to myself. I got out the pan, the milk, the vanilla, and whatever else went into the pudding, and poured these into a bowl. I cranked the hand eggbeater at least a thousand times. Standing over the bowl and rotating the eggbeater knob gave me a sense of confidence and power. I felt good watching the beaters go 'round and 'round, sending waves of milk against the side of the bowl. This cooking stuff was fun.

After beating the mixture to near exhaustion, I poured it into a saucepan and put it on a burner. The recipe said to keep stirring and let the mixture come to a "full boil," but my mentors had failed to completely explain what a "full boil" meant. As the burner heated up, I stirred my concoction. Nothing was happening, except that the mixture was getting a little warmer and little lumps were starting to form. I stirred on. It still failed to resemble any pudding that I'd ever seen. The concoction just sat in the pan and continued to lump up.

After about ten minutes, I decided that maybe it was supposed to set up in the dish, so I rounded up five Currier and Ives dessert bowls from Mother's cupboard. Filling the bowls, I carefully set one at each person's spot at the table. Surely by the time Mother returned to the house, a chemical phenomenon would have occurred and the lumps would have bonded together into a mass of luscious-looking vanilla pudding. I went about my business cleaning up the mess like a good little 4-H cook.

Mother came in from the barn. With a sense of pride, I joined her at the dinner table as she inspected the results of my first kitchen solo.

Silence. No response.

Her eyes surveyed the table, landing briefly on each bowl. More silence.

She walked to the silverware drawer and returned with a teaspoon. Dipping it into the middle of one runny pool of white lumps, she cautiously brought the spoon to her mouth. Sipping a portion, she ended her silent inspection. "What is this stuff?" she asked. "I thought you were making vanilla pudding. Why didn't it set up? Did you cook this?"

The cats got dessert that night, but the family didn't.

From that day on, Mother kept a vigilant eye on my cooking activities. I learned what effect each of the settings on the stove burners had and noticed that "simmer" definitely meant slow cooking.

We 4-Hers struggled through wienie boats, sugar cookies, and purple cows that summer. Our families struggled through the subsequent sampling. Mine always pretended that my concoctions were the most delicious delights they'd ever tasted. Of course, it didn't take much to satisfy the human vacuum cleaners Mike and Kevin. Like me, they resembled baby robins in the nest, always eager for another bite and not too fussy about its quality.

During the second year of 4-H, I expanded my domestic horizons by adding Sewing I to my slate of projects. We spent lots of time at Ella Cantrell's house working on our aprons. Ella's daughters Suzan and Kathy were 4-H veterans. They were like big sisters to me, helping as I figured out how to baste and rip out faulty seams. Ripping, I soon learned, was the 4-H sewing basic. I spent lots of hours eyeballing crooked stitches, chewing on my tongue (a family trait for anything requiring dexterity), and tugging away at the thread. We had to rip out stitches until they were right, and my apron provided fertile training ground for this much-needed skill.

By my third year, I thought I was charmed. Having successfully finished first- and second-year cooking and arts and crafts along with first-year sewing, I felt pretty good about myself. My mother had also allowed me to take her half-Arabian filly Cricket as a horse project—and bribe to keep me involved in Home Ec.

Another great event took place that year—the Delamarters moved to the country. My childhood friend Laura Delamarter had lived near us in town. When we moved to North Boyer in 1950, she still attended my birthday parties. Now we were neighbors again. The Delamarters' new home in the country belonged to Charlie Pennington. Their big, two-story white house sat in the bottomland near Sand Creek. Spring run-off usually left the house surrounded by water, but summer dried it out, and the fifty-plus acres offered all kinds of new territory to explore for yellow violets, dewberries, and wildlife. We kids loved the place because it opened up a whole new frontier for our daily fishing and swimming adventures.

Like us, Laura and her mother Eleanor became more involved in 4-H. Mrs. Delamarter was a talented seamstress and wonderful cook. She was also patient, so she assisted Lucille Hudon with the second-year sewing group. During this phase we graduated from aprons to producing an entire ensemble, including a cotton slip and a dress with full skirt, bolero, and cummerbund. I was actually excited about second-year sewing because we would make something we actually could wear to school. That, I soon learned, was easier said than done. But in early spring we started on our slips. All of us brought material to Mrs. Hudon's house, then stood in line waiting for the leaders to guide us through attaching pattern pieces to the fabric.

I knew tough times lay ahead. I'm left-handed, and the propagandists had been telling me since first grade that left-handed people couldn't do anything as well as "normal" people. They couldn't write, and they couldn't cut. We lefties had been told that so often we eventually believed it and went around making excuses anytime we were asked to perform such feats as cutting out paper dolls. "I can't cut," I'd say. "I'm left-handed."

"Oh, yes, you *do* have a problem," would be the common response. Usually I looked so pathetic that people just let me stand while they took charge of the job. It was a great cop-out; I recall that it worked at those 4-H meetings.

Once the slip material had been cut—by someone else—into its appropriate shapes, I started to work on it, basting seams in preparation for my turn at Mrs. Hudon's Singer sewing machine. Whenever I sat down at the machine, some unknown force took control. If the way I ran a sewing machine was any indication of how I'd be behind the wheel of a car, you'd never see me on the road now. To this day, I believe those sewing machines idled too fast because, when I stuck my seam under the needle and pressed on the pedal, the material raced across the surface as if it were competing in the Indianapolis 500. I seldom had time to steer the seam in the right direction. In two seconds, I had ten inches of improper stitches to rip out.

My mother inspected my project after each meeting and repeated with confidence, "Well, there's the right way, the wrong way, and the 4-H way."

And there was my way.

I was still working on attaching the straps to my flour-bag slip when the rest of the sewing club were finishing their dresses. In an effort to help me complete mine in time for the September fair, Mrs. Hudon farmed me out to Mrs. Delamarter. This was when I learned about saints. Mrs. Delamarter was not only my best friend's mother, but she was also kind and encouraging. Day after day, I walked down to her house and returned to the sewing project, which by that time occupied a permanent spot in the bedroom where she did her sewing.

As I learned to control my heavy foot on the sewing machine pedal, the sewing, ripping, sewing, ripping, sewing and ripping continued. I eventually finished the slip. By the time it was ready to be worn, every seam had been redone at least five times. At best, the generic slip would have been ugly, but mine had thousands of breathing holes to boot. Even though Mrs. Delamarter must have wondered if I was going to have to move in to finish my project, she always encouraged me, just chuckling each time I massacred another seam. Her gentle guidance kept me going, and somehow my purple-flowered dress with its black bolero and cummerbund seemed much easier than that wretched slip.

By fair time I was lucky to fit into the outfit, however. There were more reasons than friends and sewing to show up frequently at the Delamarter house. Mrs. Delamarter baked bread every day. I'd never tasted anything like it before, nor have I since. It was soft, crust and all, and melted in your mouth. Mrs. Delamarter's reputation for baking bread was known throughout the neighborhood. Dicky DeGroot, one of Kevin's friends who lived up the road from the Delamarters, used to come over occasionally and clean up their leftover toast.

Every single day of school, Laura brought tuna fish sandwiches made with Miracle Whip spread and her mother's bread. She took those sandwiches for granted. Before taking a bite, she always went through the ritual of pulling off the crust in a circular motion, so that all she had left was the heart of the sandwich, not much bigger than a silver dollar.

"What a waste!" I thought, watching her. One day I asked her for a bit of the discarded crusts. "If you're just going to throw that away, I'll eat it, " I offered.

"Sure," she said.

From that day on and for many years, I gobbled my own sandwich then finished off every bite of Laura's crusts.

So refreshments were still a highlight. Besides working day and night on my sewing in Mrs. Delamarter's bedroom, I also came once a week for the formal sewing meetings with treats. One day Mrs. Delamarter had baked a double batch of orange cinnamon rolls. When the meeting had ended, she brought a platter to the living room. Each girl took a roll. The rolls were fresh from the oven. Never had anything so delightful touched my tongue. I savored each bite, trying to make it last.

When Mrs. Delamarter offered seconds, I was the only one with gall enough to accept. "Could I have just one more?" I asked.

"Make yourself at home," she replied. "Go right ahead."

This seemed to be a licence for me to indulge my healthy appetite. So I did. I made myself at home, took another and another and several more. The other members quietly chuckled as I kept stuffing bites down my throat. A guilt twinge hit on about the sixth roll. "Are you sure it's okay?" I asked. "I just can't help it. These are the best cinnamon rolls I've ever tasted."

"Don't worry," Mrs. Delamarter assured me. "We've got another platter out in the kitchen." She probably thought I was going to quit soon.

I finally quit at thirteen—when the tray was empty. Mrs. Delamarter didn't offer any more from the kitchen, so I decided to walk home, oblivious that my gluttonous marathon had had any impact whatsoever on the Delamarter family.

Almost thirty years later, my younger brother Jim spent the night with Paul and Eleanor Delamarter in their new home in Canby, Oregon. When Jim returned to Sandpoint, he brought back a box with my name on it. I opened it. Within the wrapping sat thirteen cinnamon rolls, fresh-baked that morning. My stomach capacity and gluttony somewhat diminished, I shared.

In spite of eating too much of the Delamarters' food that summer, I did fit into my dress. I had to, because from second year on we were required to model our summer sewing project during the Friday night segment of the fair. This fashion ordeal began with a practice session where Lawana Olson, the moderator, got to know each of us and wrote a description of our outfits. Lawana had the nicest voice in the county as well as a great way of making each girl feel like she was the most special thing going. As leaders supervised, we learned what gestures to make on stage, just where to turn, and just when to delicately remove our boleros to show off our dresses. I didn't possess the pizzazz that some of the girls showed as they gracefully whirled around on stage, but I wasn't too worried. It all looked like it would be okay.

On the night of the style review, however, we faced a whole different situation. The inside arena, which was used by day for livestock showing, was packed. Pigs squealed in their pens be-neath the bleachers. Electricity filled the air. Proud parents waited.

We all changed into our outfits in the fairgrounds' home ec center and got in line on the east entrance to the arena. This was the same door that fat hogs, sheep, and steers entered on their last appearance before being loaded up to meet their maker. It seemed prophetic. As we stood waiting for Lawana to work through the style review entrants, I knew what those fat ani-mals must sense before entering the ring. Sure, all we had to do was walk in there, twirl around, remember to smile, and vanish into the night. But it seemed more like facing the executioner.

It was time.

The crop of second-year sewers stood at the door. We had to walk up a long ramp before starting our modeling routine. "And now we have Marianne Brown," Lawana's melodious, charming voice signaled, my cue to get moving. I began to trudge up the ramp. "Doesn't she look charming in her purple and black ensemble?" Lawana continued.

Some smart aleck let go with an ear-piercing whistle. It caught me off guard. My self-consciousness trebled.

I tripped, but caught myself.

The same so-called friend (fiend) let loose again. Giggles followed as I arrived at the stage. "Marianne will look smart at school this fall as she wears this cotton dress accentuated with black bolero and cummerbund," Lawana told the audience. That was my cue to remove the bolero. Walking around, trying not to trip again, while yanking off a slightly tight, goofy little jacket and ignoring the taunts of malicious adolescents required more poise than I ever had. I finally got the thing off while executing sloppy semi-military corners at each end of the stage. I tried to smile but felt more like crying as my eyes sought the quickest path off the stage and out the door. Further humiliation set in as we had to go back to receive our ribbons. Mine was a white. In 4-H they awarded blue for "the best," red for "reasonably okay" and white for "thanks for showing up." It was obvious I would never be mistaken for Cindy Crawford or Cheryl Tiegs.

I hoped the modeling disaster would be my ticket out of the home ec side of 4-H, but Mother wouldn't hear of it. "You quit home ec, you'll quit livestock," she promised. She knew I loved working with the horses and cows enough to abide by her wishes. So I grudgingly began the fourth year. By that time I had achieved veteran status among the home ec members, and Mrs. Hudon expected kids my age to strike out on more challenging pursuits. The county 4-H demonstration contest was coming up, so she recruited a couple of us for the competition.

We had been required to give demonstrations every year for each of our 4-H projects. As members got older, the content of their talks became more interesting. Beginners took on such stimulating subjects as "How to Thread a Needle," or "How to Spot a Boil." The leaders grilled us on using the correct format for our demonstrations. "You must always give your name, your age, your club name, and how many years you've taken this project," Mrs. Hudon reminded us. "At the end you must ask for questions. When the questions end, you must let them know you are finished." The content seemed secondary; if we forgot part of the format for a demonstration, Mrs. Hudon let us know about it. So we practiced it faithfully.

In fact, another member, Mary Ann John, was so faithful about learning the 4-H format that it caused her some embarrassment in church—in the confessional, to be exact. At the same time our leaders were pouring 4-H lingo into our heads, the nuns from Immaculate Heart of Mary School in Coeur d'Alene were spending two weeks each summer making us memorize Catholic prayers and the proper format for anonymously recounting our sins within the darkness of the confessional. "Bless me, Father, for I have sinned; it had been two weeks since my last confession. I accuse myself of...," had a rhythm that resembled our 4-H demonstration format. At least that's what we discovered after Mary Ann entered the confessional one day.

"My name is Mary Ann John," she told Father Dooley. "I am ten years old and a member of the Mountain View ABC Club. I have been . . ." Suddenly Mary Ann realized where she was. Suddenly Father Dooley came awake. Mary Ann decided to limit her recitation of sins that day. It's probably fortunate that the mix-up occurred in the confessional in the presence of Father Dooley and God rather than the other way around . . . with Mary Ann saying "Bless me, Father," in front of a bunch of her fellow 4-Hers.

After three years, most of us knew the demonstration format by heart and had poise enough to avoid any embarrassing slip-ups. For my cooking demonstration I decided to show my fellow members "How to Bake a Cake." I put lots of planning into my presentation, methodically unloading Mother's cupboard of flour, sugar, salt, Hershey's cocoa, and other ingredients necessary for a chocolate cake. I even remembered to take my apron along to Mrs. Hudon's house, where I stood at the kitchen table as I went through the entire operation.

Everybody loved the demonstration, mainly because I served the finished cake for refreshments at the end of the meeting. As I gathered up my props, Mrs. Hudon complimented me on what a good job I'd done. "I'd like you to take your demonstration to the county contest," she said. "I think you'd do very well."

I was honored. "Really?" I said.

"Oh, definitely," she replied. "You gave an excellent presentation. The only thing you need to do differently is measure your ingredients into smaller containers rather than bring the whole sack of flour or sugar. Do this for everything except your eggs," she continued. "You need to show that you test each egg individually before putting it into the mixture."

The proposal seemed reasonable enough to me. I liked competition, and if I did well enough at the county contest, I might go to district, which meant traveling to some other city. "Okay, I'll do it," I assured Mrs. Hudon. I was especially proud to be the only one picked from our club to participate in the county contest.

The contest was held about two weeks later at the Northern Lights Hostess Room. Mrs. Hudon picked me up, along with my three boxes of ingredients, pans, electric mixer, and spatula. I had measured flour, shortening, cocoa, milk, and sugar in separate containers, some plastic and others my mother's aluminum dry goods canisters. We walked into a packed house of 4-H leaders and nervous contestants. Mrs. Hudon and I sat down and listened to the first demonstrations. On that summer day before my seventh year of school, I met girls from other schools who would end up being close friends of mine for years.

Judy Turnbull, Peggy Broehl, Karen Arndt, and Joanne Buhr were all well-schooled in public speaking. They had the demonstration format down-pat. They even had poise enough to ad lib, "Hello!" at the start of their presentations. I was impressed, and also knew I had to put forth the extra effort if I were to give them any competition.

My turn came. I lugged up three boxes of cake essentials and carefully placed them out on the table while members of the audience visited in their respective klatches. "My name is Marianne Brown, and I'm a member of the Mountain View ABC Club. I'm twelve years old and I'm in my fourth year of cooking. Today I'm going to tell you how to bake a cake."

All conversation ended. Ladies sat at attention, and I was on my way through what I hoped would be the award-winning demonstration of the day. I started by explaining what my recipe called for. Then I proceeded to dump the basic ingredients into my bowl, all the while remembering the importance of eye contact. I found the shortening in one of the metal containers and scooped it out with the spatula. Next I measured the vanilla. "Now we add sugar," I said, reaching for another canister and surveying the audience from left to right. I have never been good at concentrating on more than one activity at a time, and I should have known better. While looking the ladies straight in their faces and droning on about how many cups of sugar were necessary, I opened the lid of the canister and dumped its contents into the mixing bowl. The audience began to giggle. I couldn't figure out why.

I started to panic. My commentary deteriorated into unintelligible, illogical mutterings. I reached for the canister containing the eggs as the ladies giggled uncontrollably. Such rude behavior was making me mad. I regained my poise and attempted to shield my disgust with an ever-present smile. Just as I was about to open the canister and explain the importance of cracking each egg into a separate bowl, I sneaked a peek at my ingredients.

Three brown eggs, shell and all, were already stuck to my shortening. It was obvious that I had made my first blooper.

"Well," I said, attempting to maintain my composure while several ladies continued to snicker. "I guess I'd better fix that." Picking each egg out, I wiped greasy shortening globs off with my spatula. Then trying not to skip a beat, recalling Mrs. Hudon's advice, I started explaining about eggs."You should always break the eggs into a separate dish before putting them into the mixture," I said, cracking each on the side of a Pyrex measuring cup. "They might be rotten or have bloody yolks." When the eggs had all passed inspection, I turned the mixer on and began the creaming process, unaware that I had forgotten to add the sugar.

Once the mixture was smooth I moved on to dry ingredients, where I took special pains to explain to the audience about level teaspoons and the importance of sifting the flour. "Now we must blend in the dry ingredients for about three minutes," I explained as the beaters began churning away at the mass of dough. "It's important to use your spatula and keep the ingredients moving for the beaters."

As the batter began to take on its chocolate color, it started climbing up the beaters. The Sunbeam mixer labored and groaned as it attempted to cut through the cementy mass, and I labored to beat the globs back down into the bowl.

More snickers. Somebody piped up, "Marianne, didn't you forget the sugar?"

"Oops," I said, stopping the mixer. "Guess I did, didn't I?"

As sweat beads from my forehead threatened to add a little more salt, I grabbed the sugar canister and quickly unloaded it into the bowl. As the mixing process resumed, the audience and I now observed exactly why certain ingredients should be added at certain times. I was forming my very own bowl of chocolate concrete. The sugar slowly blended in with the rest of the mess, and thick brown blobs began mounting the beaters as if they were trying to escape.

The hysterical ladies and my fellow 4-Hers made no attempt to stifle their glee as they watched the concoction make its gradual, persistent ascent toward the Sunbeam's main frame. Every time I'd beat it down with my spatula, the batter came back for more punishment. The mixer motor sounded like it was on its last round as the beaters wallowed through the mess. "This isn't exactly the way it's supposed to act," I said, feebly trying to must up my final ounce of composure.

Some members of the audience had their hankies out. Wiping their eyes, they were beyond listening to anything I had to say.

When my three-minute war with the cake batter ended, I

scooped the conglomeration into flour-lined cake pans, sculpted it with the spoon, and told them the importance of slamming the pans on the counter to remove air bubbles before putting them in the over. It was likely, however, that this mess had no need for further abuse. "This completes my demonstration," I said. "Are there any questions?"

They were all in such hysterics that not one could come up with even a dumb question. Finally, one empathetic lady tried to salvage the last remnant of my self-esteem. "You did a remarkable job of maintaining your composure in the face of a disaster," she volunteered, her voice rising an octave as she attempted to stifle her amusement.

I did not win the demonstration contest that day.

Meanwhile, on the sewing front, things weren't going so well either. Third-year sewing required us to build a pair of flannel pajamas with stove-pipe legs and flat-fell seams. Mrs. Delamarter had to reach deep into her bag of psychological and seamstress tricks to keep me straight when I reverted to my old ways of reckless sewing. The roadway down each leg of flannel was fraught with sneaky little snags that kept me ripping and cursing, ripping and cursing. Finally one day I brought the pajama bottoms home, and Mother decided to try to help me.

She set up the sewing machine on the kitchen table and watched in horror as I tried to stitch the three-foot-long seam without breaking another needle or destroying the sewing machine. For me, sewing was much like getting fishing line snarled in a million tiny knots. I had no patience, and when something went wrong my temper only made it worse. After watching my frustration and sensing my feelings of defeat, Mother exhibited a rare moment of sympathy. "I'll make you a deal," she began. "Just finish this project and you won't ever have to take sewing again."

My spirits lifted. I eventually got the job done, thanks again to Mrs. Delamarter's guidance throughout the rest of the summer. At the style review that fall, I smiled through Lawana's commentary about "how comfy Marianne looks in her soft pink pajamas." Ignoring the catcalls from the no-neck monster friends, I simply smiled, counting the seconds until my 4-H home ec career ended forever.

SMOKE, SMOKE, SMOKE
That CIGARETTE

As far as I know, my husband Bill has never even held a cigarette, let alone puffed on one. My children, Willie and Annie, have clean teeth, clean breath, and a clean slate in the smoking category. But I rank as one of the "most holier-than-thou" reformed sinners.

I cannot deny that I once loved to smoke. My childhood years were spent in anticipation of the day when, as a mature adult, I could sit at the kitchen table and freely light up over after-dinner conversation with Mother and Harold. The post-meal smoking scene was a daily ritual on the North Boyer farm, where the mealtime routine was fairly formal. We expected our evening meal to include beef, potatoes, vegetables, and tossed salad, topped off by a rich dessert. We learned to chew each bite of steak twenty-five times before picking up our fork and stabbing another. No elbows on the table, and no talking with a mouthful of beans. Then the art of conversation and its rules were reinforced. Although we had a black-and-white television, no one had permission to leave the table to watch it until after-dinner discussion ended. Cigarettes were necessary props for the adults during the leisurely conversations that followed our evening meals.

Virginia Tibbs
1994

Harold always got the show started. He chewed his last bite, set down his fork, turned sideways in his chair, and leaned against the wall next to the bathroom door. Once in position, he began a fascinating segment of our dinner hour: the rolling of a cigarette. No matter how often we watched the process, each night we sat mesmerized as Harold pulled the orange pack of tissue papers from his denim pocket. Separating one from the stack, he cupped it lengthwise and held it between the fingers of one hand while pulling out the bag of Bull Durham with the other. Holding the paper securely in place, he snagged the top of the bag with his teeth and pulled it open, carefully tapping its side to pour a small ridge of tobacco along the length of the paper. Clamping the little white bag's string between his teeth, he then pulled it shut and stuffed it back in his pocket. Next he carefully took the paper by both ends, licked the paper's edge, and smoothed it over the other side. A twist of one end, a tap for any stray leaves on the other, and he was ready to light up. In the meantime, Mother got her Salems and two ashtrays. After-dinner conversation could then begin.

We kids learned to listen and to contribute appropriate comments at appropriate times. The discussion usually involved stories about Harold's daily frustrations with his job at the city water department. For thirty-three years, he worked as Sandpoint's water filter operator. The low pay, long hours, and frequent problems that arose from maintaining some of the best drinking water in the United States presented plenty of conversation topics. In addition, he seldom ran short of stories about the time he spent riding forty thousand acres of range in the mountains near Montana's Madison Valley in the 1930s. These stories, as well as rehashed incidents that had happened during the day and the most recent scoop from Mother's horse friends, kept the family at the table for at least an hour every evening. Lots of talk, lots of cigarettes.

Since I spent more time listening than talking, I often occupied myself with the smoke that enveloped the table from
Mother and Harold's cigarettes. The blue-gray clouds floating
above our table provided a never-ending challenge. Sitting at
the end of the table, I often tried to grab a mouthful. I wanted
desperately to snatch some and send it back into the air as a
smoke ring. Night after night I kept the faith, knowing I would
master the elusive skill someday. Night after night the others
continued to talk as I tried to suck smoke from the kitchen air.

Taking in secondhand smoke at the dinner table didn't completely satisfy my desire to be like the grown-ups who looked so
sophisticated with their cigarettes. Still, I knew the time would
come when I could finally join their ranks and decide for myself
whether to be a Camel, Pall Mall, or Lucky Strike smoker. In
the meantime, my brothers and I concentrated on observing
Harold's skillful cigarette construction and developing a strategy for rolling our own.

On most summer days during our preteen era, we left the
house about 10 A.M. as Mother rolled out the wringer washer
and hooked the hose to the kitchen faucet. Our morning itinerary took us about a mile away to the Sand Creek bridge connecting Boyer and Highway 95. We rode our bikes and took home-
made fishing poles to go after penos, suckers, trout, or blue-
gills. In those days the creek, which originated near the top of
Schweitzer Mountain and fed into Lake Pend Oreille, teemed
with a wide assortment of fish. The boys usually pulled in at
least a dozen per day.

I was never so lucky. It was a rare day when the fish— or
my fishing equipment—cooperated. My tackle consisted of a stick
pole made from a willow or aspen tree, almost ten feet of line,
and one No. 4 hook. Hook and line usually conspired to find
some ingenious way to grab hold of a snag within the first thirty
seconds of use. Either my habitual impatience or the knowl-

edge that some mess-up was bound to happen triggered the same reaction. As soon as my hook snagged hold of the first stick, bush, or log that came into view, I jerked the pole back, pulled with all my might, uttered a few obscenities, and stomped my feet in the sand as I heard the inevitable snap that ended the day's fishing venture. Mike and Kevin always had a supply of extra hooks and sinkers in their tackle boxes, but they never cared to share with their little sister.

Fully aware that I had at least three hours to kill while the boys continued their quest for the largest lunker of the day, I found other projects around the bridge. Throwing rocks into Sand Creek lasted about as long as my fishing; with the first splash, an older brother instantly reminded me of my mortality, convincing me to consider some other pastime. "You'd better not throw another one, or I'll come over and slug you," was all the warning needed. I then wandered up the hill and began searching for ripe thimble berries or long, thick strands of timothy to chomp on. Often, leaves from the cottonwood trees suggested another activity.

"It's time to try a smoke," I sometimes decided. Ripping off several leaves, I sat down in the road, shredded the leaves into tiny pieces, and created a pile large enough to build a home-made cigarette. Then I looked for some paper to serve as a wrapper. It never took too long because that area was where pickup trucks owned by grown-up anglers parked during the evening hours. Since there wasn't much concern about the environment or many Idaho litter laws in the 1950s, these folks usually left behind an ample supply of cans, bottles, and paper for youngsters like me to gather and recycle the next day. Choosing the most likely litter for cigarette paper—with no concern for its origin, history, or germ count—I returned to my pile of leaves and attempted to copy Harold's roll-your-own technique. I never quite mastered that skill either, but my end product sort of looked and acted like a cigarette. Never mind the fact that bits of leaves dribbled out as I ambled down the road toward the bridge to ask Kevin for a match.

Kevin always had matches. They fascinated him. He always kept at least a couple of books in his pocket. After a little pleading I could usually convince him to hand over a few so I could light up my smoke. Whenever I managed to get them burning, I would fail to get much enjoyment out of my Sand Creek specials. The usual result was a few singed fingers, because most of the time only the paper caught fire while the leaves cascaded to the ground. What was left inside generally got stuck between my teeth or on my tongue as I took each puff. Occasionally, my brothers left their fishing poles propped against the yellow bridge rails and joined my attempts to enjoy a cigarette. Their efforts always matched mine.

Our disappointments at Sand Creek only fueled our need to have a good smoke. So on several occasions we resorted to what we knew best: household intrigue and creative theft. In those days we had lots of choices in the smoking department. At least five ashtrays sat on tables in the living room and kitchen, all overflowing with smashed, dried-up butts. These nicotine lovelies came in handy when the folks went to town or to visit friends. As soon as the coast was clear, we sorted through the piles and selected the stubs that still had about a quarter inch of white tissue paper extending beyond the filter. A moment or two of careful stroking to stretch and restore them to original shape produced mini-cigarettes good enough for a couple of puffs. Nothing came so close to adulthood as lounging with our legs draped over the arm of the recliners, sucking up stale smoke from dead Salems. We cherished those moments of perceived sophistication.

Kevin once had a solo smoking moment that tested his poise and tickled Harold for years afterward. Apparently my brother had felt the need to smoke a "real" cigarette out near the woods. So he filched one from Mother's pack, stuffed it under his shirt, sneaked behind the house where no one would see him, and lit up. He was in mid-drag when Harold stepped around the corner. They met face to face. Kevin had the presence of mind to put the cigarette behind his back and drop it before Harold spotted it in his hand. But he hadn't quite destroyed all the evidence.

"What are you doing, Kevin?" Harold asked.

A master of calm conviction and response in the face of trouble, Kevin gave a simple, straightforward answer. "Nothing," he insisted. He may have perfected the language to cover guilt, but Kevin had not yet learned to swallow a mouthful of smoke. The gray stream accompanying his answer and drifting into the afternoon air made Harold a bit skeptical of Kevin's veracity. The incident also led to a dinner table lecture that evening.

"Now, we don't care if you kids want to smoke," Harold began. "But we'd like you to do it here in the house with us. Just sit down and don't be shy about asking for a cigarette," he continued. "We just don't want you taking it outside where something might catch on fire." Harold tried shrewd psychological tactics to guide us away from dangerous mischief. For the most part, he succeeded—on the surface anyway. His invitation to sit down and enjoy a smoke with him and Mother went unanswered for many years. But clandestine smoking continued.

Now, we were by no means greasy-haired hoods who hung out on street corners with Luckys dangling from our lips. We prided ourselves in being more civilized than that. But as soon as we left home after our senior years of high school, each of us, without the knowledge of parents, took up the habit, which at the time seemed to be one of the symbols and privileges of young adulthood.

Mike got his start during his first year at West Point. Because of Beast Barracks and the hazing plebes endured, most of the young warriors needed some sort of pacifier to help them forget the terror that they had taken on by not attending a regular university. Within minutes of meeting us at a bus depot in Kalamazoo, Michigan, after his year-long absence, Mike begged a cigarette from Mother, who had supposedly quit a few years earlier. Unbeknownst to Harold, though, she had resumed the habit on the first day of our drive to Michigan.

"I'm going to be smoking cigarettes just on this trip," she announced as she, my two little sisters Barbara and Laurie, and I headed east on a four-day road trip to her hometown. "Since I'm the only driver, I'll need to smoke to calm my nerves," she rationalized. "When we get back home, I'll quit again. Harold is not to know."

Mother's nicotine need continued long after we returned from Michigan, but she and Mike both kept their smoking secret from Harold. I don't know what they thought would happen, unless it was that he would be terribly disappointed because of his delight when Mother had quit earlier. She and Mike reasoned that Harold really didn't need to know that the evil habit was spreading among the family. Mother went to extremes to keep her secret, hiding her Salems and getting them out only after Harold had gone to work at the filter plant. During those days she spent lots of time in the bathroom, and she always kept a fire in the stove. Whenever Harold returned unexpectedly, she could either stoke the ashes to get a little wood smoke camouflage around the house, or she could flush her cigarette down the toilet and quickly brush her teeth.

Harold didn't catch on until the "Saga of the Lonesome Butt," one Christmas when Mike was again home from West Point. Harold went into the bathroom and found a cigarette floating around in the toilet bowl. "Has Mike started smoking?" he asked Mother as she sat in the living room.

"Not that I know of," she responded. "Why?"

"Well, there's a cigarette butt floating around in the toilet," he explained. "I know it's not mine because it has a filter on it. Are you smoking again?" Unlike Kevin, Mother was not quick enough on her feet to come up with a credible response, so she confessed her deceit prematurely. Later when compelled to inspect the soggy evidence, Mother discovered that it was a Winston, not a Salem. Mike had indeed tossed the butt into the toilet and flushed it without checking to see that it disappeared from view. Once this dual deception was revealed and Mother and Mike's habits were "out of the bathroom," the trio began enjoying after-dinner smokes together.

Kevin, in the meantime, had joined the full-time nicotine crowd at his college in Pasco, Washington. Not wanting to disappoint the folks, he too kept his habit a secret for some time. However, his sin was eventually exposed—at the barrel of a rifle.

Harold's hobby has always been collecting, trading, and restoring guns. It's common for him to have an arsenal of at least a dozen hunting weapons. We learned a lot about rifles and pistols and enjoyed the stories that went with them during evenings in the living room when Harold spent hours cleaning and polishing the barrel and stock of a .30-'06 or a .22 bolt-action rifle. His tales of great guns and successful hunts fascinated us and our guests. Harold was well known for his interest in hunting and firearms. So it was not unusual that when the city crew found an 1875 Marlin rifle on an excavating job downtown, they turned it over to Harold to restore. The rifle soon became a conversation piece that hung on the wall in the living room.

Anyone inspecting the rifle for the first time was encouraged inspect it and try out the action. Harold was proud to have that gun. Finally, however, it had been admired by just about

everyone who might happen to visit, so Harold moved it upstairs and hung it on the wall next to Kevin's bed, where it remained for several months. One day another arms aficionado
came to the house, and Harold got to talking about his current
collection of guns. When the subject of the old rifle arose, he
went upstairs to get it to show to the visitor. The two men stood
in the kitchen inspecting every inch of the relic and working its
lever action. Suddenly, something dropped out of the barrel onto
the kitchen floor. It was a squashed cigarette butt.

Another followed. Harold inspected the barrel and chuckled. "H-mm, what we got here?" he commented, peering down
the cylinder. By the time he got the barrel cleaned out almost a
pack of dried-up cigarette butts lay on the floor. Virtually every
inch of the gun's barrel had been utilized as one of the world's
most unusual ash trays. Kevin's secret was literally "out of the
barrel." Once again, Harold issued an invitation, encouraging
brother number two to join the family whenever he needed a
smoke.

I followed in my brothers' footsteps and lit up my life soon
after moving into Carter Hall at the University of Idaho. My
roommate was an experienced woman who, no doubt, had been
smoking since puberty. She also had a need. She needed to get
me started as soon as possible so the two of us could share the
expense. She was also tough and smoked filterless Luckys.
Within a week, I had already sampled one of her cigarettes. Its
flavor bore a faint resemblance to our Sand Creek specials. "Just
keep with it," she assured. "You need to develop a taste. Then,
you'll like them."

I still couldn't see much fun in puffing while picking out
stray bits of tobacco from my mouth. But like a dutiful novice
who needed to earn her badge of maturity, I followed her advice.
Later, I learned that my smoking mentor's approach had a hidden agenda, borrowing the tactics of a drug dealer—show some

generosity, get 'em hooked, then take advantage. Once she knew I liked smoking she quit offering to share her cigarettes. I bought my own, but I chose to purchase L & Ms with filters. Selecting my own brand didn't quite fit with my roommate's plan.

"Those are wimpy cigarettes," she told me with an air of disgusted arrogance. "You should smoke a 'real' cigarette." Mine were wimpy until she ran out of her own supply. Then she changed her tune and begged from me.

Most Carter Hall girls started the habit as if it were one of the University of Idaho's freshman requirements. Within the first month, almost half the girls in the hall were lugging around their packs and matches. Hallways, rooms, and lounges were blue with smoke as we girls puffed openly and with pride. It was obvious that most of us were doing it for the first time in our lives. Some took quick choppy puffs, while others puffed just enough times to seal membership in the dorm's smoking sisterhood. We thoroughly enjoyed getting to know one another while sitting in the hallways basking in the thick billowy cloud created from our cooperative puff-and-blow efforts. A few cynics refused to join us, lest they go away with stinky clothing, but we just figured that sissy attitude was their problem.

As time went on, my roommate informed me that I was not getting the full value of my cigarettes. "You have to inhale," she advised me.

"I thought I was inhaling," I responded, puzzled.

"No, no, you're just taking drags and blowing them out," she explained. "You've got to breathe the smoke all the way down your throat and then let it out slowly. Do that, and you'll really get a high."

She demonstrated. It looked easy enough, but I needed to think about it for a while. Then she showed me a talent that truly separated the wusses from the pros in smoker land—French inhaling. I watched her deftly take a drag, inhaling until all smoke disappeared completely. As I was considering how Kevin could have used this skill the day Harold caught him behind the house, the grand finale came out of her nostrils in the form of two dark gray vapor trails.

"Gawd!!! How'd you ever learn that? "I marveled.

"Simple," she said. "Just takes practice."

My roommate had thus opened an exciting new frontier in my smoking world. I resolved to attempt it, but not until I was good and ready. Days passed. She continued to razz me about not inhaling. "Don't bug me," I said. "I'll do it one of these days."

One afternoon, I sat in the dorm room all by myself. My friends were either gone to their 1:00 P.M. class or lounging in the TV room watching *As the World Turns*. "Now's my chance to try inhaling," I thought while washing my hands in our counter sink and looking into one of the huge mirrors in our room. I sat down and lit up. "It's now or never," I thought to myself. Putting the cigarette to my lips, I took in a big mouthful of smoke and br-e-e-eathed in like my roomie had demonstrated.

As the smoke went down my throat my neck turned to rubber, and my head swung forward toward my chest. I released the smoke. My head w-a-a-azent that heavy, b-u-u-ut the top of it felt like someone was pu-u-u-lling ever so gently. I sat in an upright position. My head flopped back to my chest. I jerked it up again. It fell back.

Finally, regaining a little more control, I looked at myself again in the mirror. The infinity of images looking back seemed to be spinning in an up-and-down, circular motion. Slowly my wits returned. "Wow, that was something," I said, laughing at the stupid idiots that looked back and mimicked my every move. "Gotta try it again and get it perfected."

A few more drags, and my style improved considerably. My roommate could no longer heckle me. By Christmas of my freshman year I was a seasoned pro at smoking, but like all the other sneaks in my family, I didn't think it wise to go home, sit at the table, and offer Mother an L & M to go with her cup of coffee.

My coming-out party took place at the Spokane bus depot when Mother, Mary (my future sister-in-law and fellow dorm dweller), and my little brother Jim went to meet Mike. Jim, two at the time, chose that day to be terrible as we waited in the lobby. Mother decided he needed to go to the potty. Mary knew I was dying for a smoke. Waiting until Mother and Jim were completely out of view in the upstairs bathroom, she opened her purse. "Want one?" she offered.

"Oh, yes," I said, grabbing a Winston.

We lit up. Each of us took a couple of welcome drags as we discussed the inconvenience of having to keep such secrets from our folks.

"Yeah, it's a pain," I commiserated, looking up toward the balcony where Mother had taken Jim. Oops. Staring back at me was Mother with one of those "Uh huh!! Thought ya'd pull a fast one, but ya can't fool me—I gotcha" looks. I'd been had. Then she did something she'd rarely done in the long history of our mother-daughter sting operations.

She smiled.

I kept on smoking and never enjoyed a cigarette so much as that December day when guilt steadily blew away with each puff.

My smoking career lasted four years. Then, after graduating from college and becoming a full-fledged rookie teacher, I caught every illness that invaded the air space around my classroom desk. One particularly bad bout with a severe sore throat almost did me in during my first year of teaching. The pain of each swallow blocked any pleasure that might be derived from lighting up. Miserable as my sore throat was, I appreciated it because it made me quit smoking long enough to notice a difference in how I felt without morning smokers' breath and other nasty effects that came after lighting up.

I adapted a rather loose attitude about my habit. "If I quit, I quit, but if I decide to smoke again, that's okay too," I told everyone, not wanting to deal with unrealistic expectations. But being free from morning grunge mouth and the huffing and puffing involved in mere stair climbing convinced me to find other ways to satisfy my compulsions. I broke the cigarette habit in the early 1970s and don't plan to take it up again.

Good & Plentys
Won't Getcha LOVE,
but a HARMONICA WILL

I went on my first date when I was six.

We got in the car, drove to a wooded area about two miles south of Sandpoint, pulled in, and parked.

Before divulging the rest of the sultry details, I must let the reader know that my two brothers went along also. No, Mother had not sent them as chaperones to watch over their little sister. After all, it was not my date; it was hers. We had all accompanied Mother and Harold to an Audie Murphy flick at the Motor Movie, Sandpoint's finest and only drive-in theater. Had she a choice, Mother would have preferred to leave us home. However, our past history with babysitters offered her no choice.

She had been a single mom for about a year, after divorcing my real father who had a drinking problem. Since she needed to work full time, she tried to find babysitters for us, to avoid

164

latchkey problems. Ours was not a popular place for babysitters. One in particular, Mrs. Bitterich, called Mother at work and told her to come home immediately because she didn't want to deal with us anymore. We had just survived a severe bout of measles. Apparently, when we came back to life, our adrenaline levels shot up. Old Mrs. Bitterich's decision to call Mother came after Mike removed all the knobs from the electric range and hid them, which meant that Mrs. Bitterich couldn't cook us any lunch. Watching three wired (maybe even weird) kids with empty stomachs drove the woman to the brink. "You'd better come home," she told Mother. "I don't want to do this anymore."

We flunked as model children. It was not easy for Mother to find a babysitter who had the savvy to handle the likes of us, so she decided it was a lot easier to just take us along when she struck up a romance with Harold Tibbs, the nice guy who lived down the road at the Racicots'. As a member of the Sandpoint Saddle Club, Mother had become good friends with Ardis Racicot. Since we spent a lot of time at the Racicots' house, she got to know Harold better and better. In fact, we all started seeing more of him as he came to our place to help with hay, fences, and animals. Harold and Mother soon began their courtship.

Harold came to pick all of us up in his maroon 1949 Ford sedan named "Whoopie." He and Mother sat snuggled in the front seat while we three kids sat in the back. Cars loaded with hyper teenagers surrounded us. The movies always rated a PG, as did the action in the front seat. With three young chaperones watching their every move, the new couple had no choice but to behave. Harold passed our test, and we must have passed his, since he didn't let our presence stop him from marrying Mother.

Mother and Harold drove ninety miles to Thompson Falls, Montana, to tie the knot. Their wedding took place March 12, 1954, in the Sanders County Courthouse, under the direction of the town's Justice of the Peace—also owner of the Ford garage.

Not surprisingly, they chose not to bring us along for the wedding and honeymoon.

A few years after their marriage Mother began counseling me with tips about the type of man to seek as a mate. In the 1950s, mothers dreamed of the day when their daughters would find just the right young man, marry, and live happily ever after as a dutiful housewife. "Marry a rich man," she had repeated on several occasions. I don't know why she felt this was a priority, but I do know she was not unique in her approach; every female friend I've had throughout my lifetime has heard the same words.

Nevertheless, I took her advice to heart when I went to the seventh grade and began a serious search for the right mate. When I discovered that Gregory McFarland sat next to me in reading class I knew I'd hit pay dirt early on. Gregory's parents owned one of the largest cedar pole companies in the Northwest. Rumor had it they were rich, so I set my sights toward enchanting him. Gregory was a rather timid boy. He had a studious, collegiate look with his glasses and Ivy League vests. He spent most of his time with his nose in a book, but whenever he came up for air I greeted his glance with a generous, adoring smile.

I also observed, after skillfully tracking him around school for a week, that my potential rich husband enjoyed a daily package of Good & Plentys from the Whatnot Shop, our hangout and candy shop across from the junior high. "The surest way to a man's heart is through his stomach," Mother had said in her marital advice lectures. I knew that if I were to catch Gregory's romantic attention, I was going to have to part with some of my loose change and bait him with a gift of Good & Plentys. "If you're going to make money, you have to spend money," I thought.

So I scooted out of literature class one noon hour and hurried across Pine Street to be the first in line at the candy counter.

Taking my dime, Mrs. King, the proprietor, reached into the glass case, pulled out the lavender and white box, and handed it to me. I sped out the door, handing him the candy. "I noticed you like these and thought I'd buy you some."

With a puzzled expression, he uttered a quick "Thanks," took the Good & Plentys, and went on his way. I repeated the gift-giving three more times. Gregory always accepted the candy and ate it. However, he never went out of his way to initiate any conversations with me.

"It'll come," I reasoned. "He'll appreciate my generosity and do the right thing when it really counts."

It counted one night at a seventh grade dance. This affair differed from the weekly Friday noon dances in the gym. At noon the jukebox blasted out Connie Francis and Everly Brothers singles while virtually all the females at Sandpoint Junior High gyrated around the gym in the "Twist" or the "Mashed Potato." Meanwhile, virtually every boy in the school vegged out on the bleachers with a deadpan expression. Not one could be pried from his spot. The evening dances, which came three or four times a year, had the advantage of a darkened gym. Like owls, many boys became social creatures in the dusky light. Some actually mustered up enough nerve to ask a girl to dance. Occasionally it was girls' choice, so no one had an excuse to go home moping.

I had high hopes that my investment in Good & Plentys would pay off during this first real dance. Crepe paper streamers hung from all sides of the gym; faculty chaperones stood in a corner, sipping punch from the refreshment table. The gym was dimly lit, but not so dark as to obscure the view of young eyes looking for love. My optimism soared when I spotted Gregory walking into the dance, surveying the crowd through his scholarly spectacles. All the boys sat in the bleachers on one side of the gym facing the girls on the other. Gregory chose a spot directly across the gym from me. "He's got to be planning his move," I thought. "He's looking at me."

The jukebox played "Put Your Head On My Shoulder." Gregory rose from his seat and walked a straight line in my direction. My ecstatic heart beat wildly as visions of pink and white Good & Plentys made me smile. I had my man. He came closer with a determined expression—a man on a mission—and was just a couple of feet away as I began planning some small talk for our slow dance. He stood almost directly in front of me, extended his hand, and asked——Karen Arndt, who was sitting beside me.

As the two walked hand in hand to the dance floor, my heart sank, my body slumped, and all my thought processes went off the air. It was more than my mind could fathom. My plan had been perfect and seemed to be working so beautifully until that moment, when I realized that Good & Plentys would never be enough to buy love. Gregory eventually left Sandpoint Junior High School and transferred to a private school in Spokane. I saw him only occasionally after that and he never really warmed up to me. I haven't purchased a box of Good & Plentys since.

It took some time to get over the Gregory affair, but I eventually resumed the search for Mr. Right. There weren't a lot of other rich men at Sandpoint Junior High School, so I lowered my standards. All they needed to do was breathe and notice my existence. These new requirements opened a vast horizon of possibility, but I was still alone on the range of romance for several months.

Cupid brought me a hot prospect at the Bonner County Fair the following summers. The fair, once the biggest event in Bonner County, signaled the end of summer. My brothers and I lived for the fair because we loved both the 4-H competition and the chance to meet new friends from Priest River and Clark

Fork. We took our animals to the 4-H barn, got them settled, then set off to explore the grounds, searching for new faces and new exhibits. After chasing around the barns and darting to and fro among the shiny new John Deer and New Holland farm implements, many young men and young women got down to the truly serious business of the fair: selecting new beaux from the faraway town twenty miles away. The flames of love began to burn long on Friday afternoon, halfway through the fair. Much work needed to be done over the next day and a half to insure that a romance was sealed well enough to receive a love letter to show friends.

That year I snagged a live one from Priest River. Larry Edgar was tall, blond, and charming, and he noticed back. He started hanging around our livestock barn a lot. I giggled at all his comments. He told me how nice my cow looked. That evening a bunch of us decided to walk from the fairgrounds through the adjoining city park to watch the high school football game at Memorial Field. As we left the lights of the fairgrounds behind, Larry made his move—only to find he had selected a dummy from the lot.

"Is your hand cold?" Larry asked me.

"Huh?" I replied.

"Is your hand cold?" he repeated.

"No," I said. I was a very literal person and my hand was actually sweating at the time. It took me a few minutes to wake up to the fact that Larry really wanted to hold my hand. Farm girls had lots to learn in the love department. Nonetheless, by the time the fair ended, Larry had declared that I was his girl-friend. We promised to write, knowing we must part for an entire year until another fair rolled around.

I received letters from Larry—and his mother. Seems she took a liking to me, too. I was pretty flattered, but *my* mother thought it was a bit odd that Larry's family had gotten so involved with our fair time romance. "I wouldn't get too serious," she warned. "You've got to finish your education." She became even more concerned after the yearlong safety net fell by the wayside when I wrote and asked Larry to the Sadie Hawkins dance. Mother felt relieved when he called a week before the dance and said he couldn't make it because he'd broken his arm. I, on the other hand, became desperate. Everyone was going to the Sadie Hawkins dance because the girls could ask the boys. With my ace in the hole gone, I would have to work overtime to find a date.

One day in literature class I spied an unsuspecting victim: Dennis Timoskevich. He was so shy that he wouldn't even look at girls, let alone talk to them. It was a sure bet that no one had asked Dennis to the dance. I wasted no time. I followed him out of the room and caught up with him in the crowded hallway. "Oh, Dennis, would you like to go to the Sadie Hawkins dance with me?" I inquired.

"No," he said, without batting an eye. It was as if he had anticipated the request and had rehearsed the most emphatic, clear "no" that had ever been uttered.

I was floored. Two rejections in one week. Sadie Hawkins Day was for the birds. I just wouldn't go to the dance if I had to go as a single. My friends, however, convinced me to swallow my pride and show up.

Lucky I did. When Mother dropped me off at the junior high, I walked up the steps and spotted a tall blond beaming from ear to ear. It was Larry. He had decided that a little broken arm wasn't going to stop him from seeing his Bonner County Fair sweetheart. We had a relatively nice time at the dance, but somehow the sparks that flew among the livestock, the food booths, and the city park trees had become dying embers over the past few months. After the dance we said good-bye, each knowing we would go to next year's fair looking for new and different love. Our summer romance had fleeted with the autumn leaves.

Mother used the term "summer romance" years later when I met the true love of my life on the shores of Lake Pend Oreille. I was on my own by then, living in the Pine Trailer Court where the Motor Movie of my six-year-old first date had stood, and working as a schoolteacher. I was also working as a feature writer for the *Sandpoint News Bulletin*. My editor Gary Pietsch had assigned me the job of writing a tabloid paper full of features about the 1973 Boy Scout Jamboree.

On one occasion, while interviewing a bagpipe-playing Scotsman named Angus McBride about what went on in the Trading Post Warehouse, I suddenly became aware of a presence surrounding me. Looking up from my pad, I found at least a dozen nice-looking young men plopped in various chairs around the tent where I sat. As I acknowledged their presence and took a break from the interview, they began to quiz me on just who I was and where I lived.

"I'm from Sandpoint," I answered. "I teach at the high school there."

That was their cue to ask the important question. "What are the girls like in Sandpoint? Are they as good-looking as the girls in Coeur d'Alene?" one asked.

Civic pride set in. "Of course they're as good-looking as the girls in Coeur d'Alene," I boasted. "They're better looking. I know because I'm the drill team adviser."

"Can you get us dates?" another asked. By then, I'd heard enough questions to know I was dealing with a herd of Southern gentlemen. I was charmed. They were all nice-looking and polite. Besides, they were Boy Scouts; they *had* to be nice.

"Of course," I bragged. "Are any of you twenty-five?" I wasn't going to waste all this potential on my drill team girls. Certainly someone in the group would be a good match for me.

One hand slowly rose in the back. He hadn't uttered a word so far.

The conversation went on a few more minutes. By the time I left, a dozen young strangers had put in their orders for dates. I had even given them the names of some of the girls on my drill team. Their spokesman, a young man from Texas A & M, said he would keep in touch. Driving back to Sandpoint, I beamed, basking in the idea of what a nice interview it had turned out to be.

Many of my drill team girls were on my softball team, and we had a game that night. I arrived, jumped out, and shared the news. "They're so nice and good-looking, and they're all Southern gentlemen," I reported. "And they want dates. How many of you would like dates?" Almost immediately I had half a dozen takers. Later that evening, Holly, a self-appointed spokesperson for the drill team contingent, called to say her mother had offered their house as a setting for the mass date. We could all play pool in the family room. The Whitakers had a beautiful house on the bank of the Pend Oreille River with ample room for a couple of dozen young people. Helen Whitaker's generosity showed she was no dummy. If her daughters were going to hook up with some blind dates, she was going to supervise.

That night after the game, when I went home, sanity returned. "What have I done?" I thought to myself. "I'm supposed to be an upstanding school teacher, not the head of the local dating service. What are the parents going to think? What will the community think if it ever gets wind of this?" Hardly sleeping—tossing, turning, and thinking about the bind I'd gotten myself into—I resolved midway through the endless night to stop this nonsense. "Yeah, when Mr. Texas A & M calls, I'll tell him I couldn't get any girls to go," I reasoned. "The girls will just have to assume that nobody called." I had come up with the perfect plan to get out of this dilemma, so I finally drifted off to sleep.

Mr. Texas A & M didn't call. Two days later, I was feeling pretty safe when the phone rang. It was Holly. Mr. Texas A & M had remembered her name and contacted her instead. The dates were set. Holly had done the match-making. She had assumed control of the entire operation. A low feeling consumed me. "Oh, no," I thought. "This thing's gotten out of control." Besides, I'd lost out completely. Twelve of my drill team girls had dates for Saturday night, and I had come out of the deal with nothing but a giant burden on my soul. I would lost my job as a teacher because of my irresponsibility.

On Friday evening I was sitting in my trailer stewing about the situation when the telephone rang. "Marianne, this is Bill Love," the nice Southern voice said. "I'm one of the guys you met at the Trading Post the other day. I'm in charge of those young men, and I just called to assure you that I will be accompanying them when they come to Sandpoint tomorrow night. You don't need to worry about a thing. They won't behave like a bunch of troops heading in for a big night on the town. They will be gentlemen."

I had just heard the most welcome words ever. This man was psychic. He knew my concerns and allayed my fears. A huge wave of relief swept over me as he continued.

"Are you coming with the girls?" he asked.

"Well, I guess I could," I said. "Why?"

"I'd like you to," he replied with the charm of a true Southerner.

"Which one are you?" I asked.

"I'm the one who's twenty-five," he responded. "I'm from Louisiana."

"Hmm, the quiet one," I thought. "Guess he's not so quiet . . . and he's so charming." All was well with the world. The big date was going to be okay. My teaching job was once again secure. Mothers needn't worry about their daughters. And best yet, I had myself a nice date, too.

The plan was to meet at City Beach. All dozen girls showed up, eager to see the Prince Charming clones I had described that night at the softball game. We stood around looking like pickups (female, that is) for about half and hour before two cars finally pulled up to the curb and parked. As the guys got out, the girls stood silently staring. The herd of young men approached, with Bill leading. He introduced each member of his group. I introduced mine.

The girls didn't move. The guys stood in a clump. Bill and I talked, stopping long enough to observe that not a lot of bonding was going on. We decided to go to the Whitakers' house. Once there, the boys played pool in the family room as the girls sat and watched politely. Bill and I continued to talk, all the time wondering when anyone else would follow suit.

To warm things up a bit, Helen summoned all of us to the beach below the house, where that afternoon the family had gathered driftwood for a huge bonfire. We all left the family room to gather around the huge, snapping flames. Girls and boys finally started pairing off. I beamed. Bill pulled a Marine Band harmonica from his pocket and began to play "Shenandoah." As the notes wafted through the warm July air, I thought, "This is what it's all about—a bonfire, good friends, a nice man, and beautiful music."

The one-man concert continued for about fifteen minutes, capped off by Bill's rendition of Beethoven's Ninth Symphony, better known as the "Ode to Joy." It might as well have been "Ode to Love," because I had fallen. "I can deal with the guy for the rest of my life," I thought.

We said good-bye on the Whitakers' porch that night with plans for tennis the next day. Tennis was followed by walks along the beach, hikes through the woods at Priest Lake, and lots of moonlight strolls along Lake Pend Oreille near Farragut where Bill was camped for the Jamboree. Sometimes our dates ended with a drive into that same wooded area two miles north of Sandpoint where we had accompanied my parents so many years before. We would pull in, park, then say good night, and I would walk in to my rented trailer.

The Jamboree ended, and Bill headed back to Louisiana. I was to accompany a group of kids to a judging contest at the National Youth Horse Congress in Dallas, Texas. As fate would have it, Bill and I had been scheduled on the same flight. When Bill leaned this, he suggested that I take a Louisiana side trip when the contest ended.

When I mentioned my plans to Mother, she seemed concerned about such a big move after just a two-week relationship. "Oh, Marianne, that's just a summer romance," she assured me. "It'll never last."

I don't know how long it takes to determine that summer romances have fizzled, but Bill and I have enjoyed twenty years of marriage—and a host of harmonica classics.

MARIANNE'S
Left-Handed APPROACH
to LIFE'S CHALLENGES

One recent summer day, while driving home from town, I pulled into our driveway and discovered that my most beautiful rose bush ever had been blown down by a brisk wind. Gasping and groaning, I parked the van, got out, and walked to the five-foot stem lying on the grass near the corner of the house. A giant hot-pink blossom dropped petals as I pulled the stem to the upright position. I could see that the stem wasn't completely severed. "Well, maybe there is a chance I can save this thing," I thought, proceeding to the house in search of duct tape. Prying

loose a six-inch strip, I cut it off and returned to the fallen rose bush. After propping up the stem and snubbing it to a piece of plastic pipe that had supported my tomato vines, I tightly wrapped the piece of tape around the area where the bush had almost broken off. Then I watered the rose and prayed. The last time I checked, its leaves were drooping and its expectant buds were sagging.

I doubt that any rose doctor worth his salt would ever suggest such a method for salvaging a dying plant. In fact, I don't think many experts would concur with most of my methods for solving problems and meeting life's challenges. My ways may be strange, but they've taught me some valuable lessons that have guided me through my adult years and kept me surprisingly stable.

I've always walked to a different beat than others, and have many times attempted the insane. I don't know why. Maybe it's my left-handedness. I read recently that left-handers are accident prone because they get sidetracked easily. More study may someday show that we southpaws really have extra brain connectors that every once in a while don't get the messages through, thus causing us to behave and approach life in a somewhat bizarre fashion. That would explain a lot for me.

My loony career began early on our North Boyer farm. I remember one incident in particular. We always had horses, and they often served utilitarian purposes. When Mother was a single parent, she had no car. When we didn't go to town by taxi, we sometimes rode horseback. Mother had our meat stored at Jack's Lockers in the north residential district of Sandpoint about three miles from our home, so occasionally she rode to town and back, bringing home a supply of steaks and hamburger in her saddlebags. One time she decided to take me along.

I was about five years old at the time, and my job was to sit, hold on to the saddle horn, and be quiet while Mother on her horse led Darkie, her black quarter horse gelding and my mount, by a long halter rope. I did precisely as I was told and kept my mouth shut as the horses clip-clopped down Boyer toward the lockers. But we hadn't gotten too far before my saddle began to slide off to one side. I kept quiet, though, because I knew Mother well enough to do exactly as I was told. I could feel myself slowly slipping more and more and attempted to wiggle the saddle back to its proper position, but, during that rare time in my life, I didn't weigh enough to reseat it. The Western saddle insisted on following its downward path, and my perspective offered a whole new view of the world. By the time Mother turned around to see how I was doing, my head and upper body were almost parallel to the ground. The saddle had slid about ninety degrees due east, and was continuing its journey down under.

"What in the world?" she screamed, jumping off of Largo. "Why didn't you tell me the saddle was slipping?"

"You told me to be quiet," I replied innocently. At the time I had a one-track mind, or maybe one of my brain connectors had gone bad. All I knew was that my job was to keep quiet. She hadn't instructed me to do any thinking. What could she expect?

Mother pushed the saddle back on top of Darkie, tightened the cinch, and on we went to get the meat. After that experience I learned to be a little more assertive in the face of danger, but it was a long time before she invited me to join her on the equestrian meat run again.

As time went on I acquired the ability to think for myself and turned into a rather enterprising young lady, willing to take on projects most girls my age wouldn't consider. I rather liked scrounging for freebies. Many of my summer hours were spent walking the ditches in search of salable beer and pop bottles. My enthusiasm became contagious among my family members. Mother and Harold would occasionally help out if they happened to spot a pile of bottles, which they eventually coined "Mariannes."

"There's a Marianne," Harold would say, bringing the car or pickup to a halt. I'd jump out, gather it, and add it to my gunny sack depository in the wood shed. When I needed money or if the sack was full, we'd load up and go down to the bottling company near the Northern Pacific railroad depot to make the big transaction. I usually would leave with a couple of dollars' worth of spare change.

I found other riches in the neighborhood ditches. About the middle of July in our part of the country, dewberries ripened. Every other morning for about two weeks, I took off with a fruit jar and fought through stickers and garter snakes to pop off big, black berries. After about an hour of picking and covering about a mile's worth of dusty ditches along Boyer and the back road, I returned with about half a pint of berries and plenty of new scratches on my legs. When we got enough, Mother baked a pie. The berries were seedy, but they had a delicious taste all their own which we really appreciated, since dewberries were not very abundant. Dewberry pie was a treat we dreamed of all year long.

My annual dewberry project and my constant search for "Mariannes" set my entrepreneurial desires in high gear. My sense of perseverance and belief that financial success could be attained through patience, vision, and willingness to strike out on my own inspired me to get involved in the annual *Sandpoint News Bulletin* subscription drive contest. The owners of the newspaper gave away bicycles, money, and trips to Disneyland. Each year huge pictures of contest winners were featured on the front page of the weekly paper. I saw this as my opportunity to enjoy the good life and receive fame among the Sandpoint readers besides.

As a sixth grader, I decided to enter the contest, which began right after school had ended. It ran through most of June. I went to the *Sandpoint News Bulletin* office and met with Max Poulter, the middle-aged promoter who came every year to coordinate the contest. He explained that our mission was to cover zones within the Sandpoint area and sell subscriptions—lots of them. Max gave me a booklet along with tips for my sales approach and wished me good luck. With visions of a vacation to Disneyland in my head, I initiated my campaign at a natural venue, our living room.

"Hi, I'm Marianne Brown, and I'm selling subscriptions to the *Sandpoint News Bulletin* ," I announced to my folks. "Would you like to buy one? I'm trying to earn a trip to Disneyland." My maiden sales attempt worked. My parents bought. After hitting up family friends like the Crocketts, the Whites, and the Lines, I struck out for the trenches. My assigned area was the northern part of town. Knocking on door after door, I repeated my spiel over and over. "Hi, my name is Marianne Brown; I'm selling subscriptions to the *Sandpoint News Bulletin*. Would you like to buy one? I'm trying to earn a trip to Disneyland." The door-to-door experience taught me lessons about rejection and the numerous excuses and creative methods people will use to say no.

Occasionally, however, I'd land a hot one who actually bought a subscription. I was competing with twenty-five other kids throughout town, so I knew my transactions would not come easy. Each time I filled out a sales slip and receipt was a personal triumph. "Max will be proud of me when I meet with him this week," I thought. He must have known the difficulties we faced, however, since when I checked in and dejectedly handed over just two receipts, he lifted my spirits with another carrot to send me back into action. "I've got a hot customer for you," he said. "Here's the telephone number and here's where they live. They're expecting you." His inside scoop was just the medicine I needed to trudge onward toward the dream of actually meeting

Mickey Mouse and Donald Duck. The easy sale revived my self-confidence. I could now knock on more strangers' doors and repeat my sales pitch another hundred times, meeting with rejection another ninety-nine.

My efforts to win the *News Bulletin* contest consumed my life and temporarily affected my psyche. One night I dreamed I was knocking on a new door, meeting a new customer. "Hi, I'm Marianne Brown," I told the imaginary face. "I'm selling subscriptions to the *Sandpoint News Bulletin*. Would you like to buy one? I'm trying to earn a trip to Disneyland." My dream, however, was stranger than I thought. I became aware of that fact the next morning when my parents asked me if I'd been having problems in the middle of the night.

"Why?" I asked.

"Well, because you were yelling at us," Mother responded.

"Huh? What do ya mean?"

"First you yelled, 'Mother and Harold?'" she explained. "When we answered, you asked, 'Do you have a good bed?'" She told me they had responded that they indeed had a very good bed. Then they had asked why I wanted to know.

"I just wanted to know if you had a good bed," I yelled back at them. End of sleep talk.

Working twenty-four hours a day trying to sell *News Bulletin* subscriptions didn't pack it against my competitors who had the luxury of several hundred soft-hearted relatives who could spring for another year of the local paper. When the contest ended, I did not go to Disneyland. I did not ride a new Schwinn Flyer home. Instead, I stuffed a ten, a five, and two ones into my wallet. My commission for selling about twenty subscriptions added up to seventeen big ones for me. Still, that was a substantial wad, a mint compared to the nickels and dimes I was accustomed to earning from my bottles. In fact, I was so proud of it, I carried the wallet full of money in my pocket wherever I went—even to the Delamarters, who lived north of us on Sand Creek.

Pride went before my fall.

Although Laura Delamarter, my best friend, had moved to the country a few years before, she and her family had not spent much time around farm animals. They had a black mare appropriately named Blackie. None of them had the nerve to ride her because she would rear straight up on her hind legs on command. So the Delamarters welcomed my willingness to exercise the horse. Since riding without supervision was restricted at home, I knew I'd found a good deal when my friends gave me permission to ride Blackie any time I wanted.

One day soon after earning my *News Bulletin* windfall, I went for a ride on Blackie. On previous occasions, I had learned the right cue to get the mare to rear. A simple tug upward on both reins and she would stand up on her hind legs, reaching for the sky with her front hooves—just like in the movies. I had ridden bareback illegally on enough Holstein calves and horses to know just how to grip her ribs and avoid slipping off. My usual sessions with Blackie included galloping at high speed down the trails and up the hillsides along Sand Creek, all the time pretending I was a Wild West cowgirl. When you're racing away from rustlers, occasionally your mount gets a little riled up. That's when I'd cue Blackie to rear. Then, we'd take off again through the woods. On that particular day, I finished my ride, put Blackie up, and headed home.

The next morning when I slipped into my jeans I noticed my wallet was missing.I quietly looked all over the room and throughout the house. No luck. That's when it dawned on me that the wallet must have fallen out while I was riding Blackie. I went down to the Delamarters' to search. Again, no luck. Depression set in, but I couldn't tell anyone. They had warned me.

"If I were you, I wouldn't be flashing that money around

for everyone to see," Mother had advised. "You're either going to lose it, or someone will steal it."

The advice had gone in one ear and out the other. I was certainly capable of keeping track of my money. When Mother's prediction came true, I vowed that she would be the last to know.

About three days after losing the wallet and during what we called "Starvation Week," (the last week before payday) Mother came to my room. "Marianne, you don't suppose I could borrow about five dollars from you, so I could go buy some bread, baloney, and Miracle Whip?" she inquired.

Gulp. "Well, sure," I said.

She stood waiting.

"I've got to get it," I said, hoping she would go comb her hair or apply her lipstick while I sneaked out the front door, never to be seen again. But she didn't comply. She just stood there, innocently waiting for the cash advance. I opened the top drawer of my dresser and pretended to search for the wallet. "Well, gosh, it's not in here," I said. "Must be in another drawer." I opened the next one down and dug through my underpants and socks. "Not in here either—hmm, I wonder where it is," I mumbled, feigning disbelief.

She started getting suspicious.

I opened the drawers until there weren't any more to open. Mother folded her arms and assumed the "Okay, what's going on here?" pose. I got down on all fours and looked under my bed. The perennial sweat rivers were rushing off my brow. I'd been found out. I knew it, and by now, Mother was ninety-nine percent sure. Deciding the charade wasn't fooling anyone, I abruptly stopped my search and stood up. "I don't have the money," I confessed. "It's gone. I lost it the other day while I was down at the Delamarters' riding Blackie."

My confession done, Mother dished out the expected penance. "What did I tell you about carrying that money around with you? Didn't I tell you? But, no, you knew better, didn't you?" she snapped. "Now, you've lost your money, and we won't have any bread or Miracle Whip until payday!" Those were grim words around our house, where Miracle Whip sandwich spread and bread were family staples and, in fact, still are. "You will go down to the Delamarters', and you will find that wallet!" she ordered. I don't know which had set her off the most—my ignoring her advice, my pretense of looking for the wallet that I knew was nowhere near my bedroom, or the knowledge that Starvation Week was going to be tougher than usual.

I scooted out the door and hot-footed it down to Delamarters where a surprise awaited me. Since I last had searched, a bulldozer had come in and turned over huge mounds of dirt in most of the areas where I could have dropped my wallet. Nonetheless, I scoured the woods in a fruitless effort. The wallet never did turn up, though, and it was several years before I ever again earned seventeen dollars at one time. From that day forward, I took better care not to flash my cash.

Such lessons kept popping up throughout our relatively carefree years as preadolescents. Mother and Harold always allowed us our independence as long as we honored a few basic rules of courtesy. "Let us know where you're going and be back at a reasonable time" was one of their standards. During our early years, my brothers and I left almost every morning after finishing our chores to spend most of the day down at the Sand Creek bridge, fishing. As we got older, we branched out and each did our own thing. We always seemed to learn about our own shortcomings through the trouble we found on our personal adventures. We also learned to think on our feet, discovering that people don't always give you a fair shake.

During the summers of our early teens we aimed our bikes toward City Beach almost daily. By that time it had become important to my brothers that we not be seen together, lest anyone know that Mike and Kevin were related to Marianne. They reminded me of this often to make sure I didn't get any bold notions of accompanying them anywhere in public. So, each day after allowing them a head start, I'd leave the driveway on the four-mile ride to the beach for an afternoon of fun with friends in the cool, clean waters of Lake Pend Oreille.

The ride became routine, until my bike started having a problem. The left pedal kept falling off, so I screwed it back as tightly as possible. Eventually, the threads became stripped, so I had to wire the pedal to the bike. I used a good supply of Harold's thin wire each day and wound it snugly around, through, and every other possible direction to hold the pedal in place. By the time I got to town, however, the pedal and the wire had worked loose. Without any warning, my left foot slapped the pavement as the pedal dangled like a bird's broken wing.

This happened just a couple of blocks from the beach, so I walked the bike, parked it, and worried about how I was going to get home later. After three hours of diving off the dock and sunbathing with friends, I got the dismal feeling that the four-mile walk pushing my bike wasn't going to be fun. In a desperate attempt to pretend that just maybe it would really work this one time, I wrapped up the broken pieces of wire and tried to snub the pedal back to its frame. My Band-Aid approach was successful for about one block.

Cuss words flew, and my temper went into overdrive as I retrieved the errant pedal, held it along with my handlebars, and resumed riding the bike by pushing the right pedal in the usual fashion and manipulating the empty left pedal frame with the toe of my shoe. I stomped it downward, then stuck my toes underneath to push it upward. The process was awkward at best. Not only did it look stupid to passersby, it also took twice the amount of time to get home. My desire to go to the beach each day, however, led to continued creative attempts to find new ways to wire the pedal and frame together.

My methods never worked. The bike finally went to a fix-it shop, never to be seen again. We waited for months to get it back; all we ever got was stories about why the repairman just hadn't gotten around to it yet. Later I learned from his blabber mouth son that the repairman *had* gotten around to it. He had used my bike for parts on other bicycles that came into his shop. We never pressed the issue, and I never pressed pedals to the beach again, except for occasional days when my brothers loaned me their bikes.

My tendency toward the bizarre approach to life has not gone away since those days of horses, bikes, and wallets. I continue to learn and to suffer loose brain connections when facing day-to-day obstacles. But let's face it: if left-handers do live shorter lives, we might as well make our numbered days interesting.

BATCH TWO

When people mention slumber parties I think of babies and Joanne Buhr. I got acquainted with all three in the seventh grade. I have no regrets.

Leaving Lincoln School in 1959 meant saying good-bye to recess and playgrounds. It seemed like a good trade-off, however, because Sandpoint Junior High School opened the door to new freedoms and independence. I was excited about the changes junior high would bring to my life, and when the summer came I started counting the days until I could remain on the bus headed for Pine and Euclid Streets, gloating while unfortunate little tykes still had to get off at Lincoln.

About midway through the count-down, I learned of another up-coming major change in

our family that would involve marking days off the 1959 calendar. We were seated around the kitchen table one summer evening when the after-dinner conversation departed from horses, water department problems, and farming to a topic that would keep our minds spinning for months afterward. "There're going to be some changes around here," Mother announced. "You're going to have a new little sister or brother in a few months."

The usual post-dinner daydreaming suddenly ceased. Kids shifted in their chairs and sat at full attention, listening to Mother's every word and eyeing her with a whole new perspective. "When?" one of us finally blurted.

"In late December," she responded. Mother did not yet show the physical signs of pregnancy, but from that day forth she would be closely scrutinized by three sets of eyes.

We were told about our new roles in the picture as older, responsible siblings. Mother and Harold also discussed how some of our household arrangements would be changing, and spoke about plans for an addition to the house. All the while, we sat dumfounded.

After drying the dishes that evening, I went outside to collect my thoughts about the big news. Kevin walked by and quietly announced a meeting, scheduled for the next afternoon at the broken-down Sand Creek bridge across the Bests' field. In spite of our sometimes adversarial sibling relationship, we occasionally held informal conferences about family issues. This was the big one.

The next afternoon, rather than go to the beach, we set out on different paths leading to the same location down the hill from the Bests' field for a clandestine meeting. A well-beaten path wound down the hillside through five-foot-tall grass, and branched out in several directions around the remaining huge beams and pilings of the derelict wooden bridge that had served as a main creek crossing decades before. Local fishermen and the Bests' Holstein cows had kept the paths open over the years. It was a quiet spot, though the cacophony of crows occasionally mixed with the euphony of summer songbirds in their temporary homes. Highway 95 ran north and south along the other bank, and only the occasional roar of logging trucks barreling through on their way to local lumber mills reminded us of the hectic world outside our Sand Creek sanctuary.

On that particular day, Kevin straddled one of the abandoned beams like a bronc rider. Mike and I plopped below him in deep grass. "Well, what do you think?" Kevin asked, as he presided over the meeting. Our decision was unanimous—it was good news, and we couldn't wait until the new arrival. I was relieved to no longer be referred to as the "baby" of the family, since that had always given me the notion that nobody would ever take me seriously as a young adult. We took bets on whether it would be a girl or a boy. I preferred a new little sister, even if she would be almost thirteen years younger, but we agreed that either would be okay.

Summer passed. One of my countdowns ended as friends and I went to Merwin's Hardware to purchase our $1.98 combination locks for our first-ever school lockers. We would have lots of books to lug from class to class, and a myriad of new names to learn when we met our six new teachers and a host of new classmates. When school opened that September I spotted Joanne Buhr, whom I'd met at a county 4-H demonstration contest. As we continued to get acquainted, she told me that her mother was going to have a baby also. Joanne and I seemed to have a lot in common, and we became friends.

Except for a few romantic disasters, I liked the seventh grade. The step up to junior high provided many of us our first chance to rebel against the system. Some kids wear earrings in their nose; others dye their hair florescent green. We abandoned the Palmer method.

Our Lincoln School principal, Marvel Ekholm, had strictly enforced penmanship rules and had closely monitored our writing style. In fact, she and her team of elementary instructors guarded our penmanship with the tenacity of the Hanes underwear inspector. If a kid had the audacity to modify the slant of his or her writing from the accepted forty-five-degree angle to the right, the teacher would make an example of the nonconformist. This chastisement usually quelled future attempts to depart from accepted standards, but fed our secret determination to get 'em back on the first day of junior high. Within days of entering the seventh grade, lots of us quit looping our *g*s and *y*s and wrote backhand. Teachers didn't care. It was our break with adult-imposed conformity, so with each stroke of improper penmanship we symbolically thumbed our noses at Mrs. Ekholm, Mr. Palmer, and anyone else who set themselves up as the official experts on cursive writing.

Besides being a rebel with a pen, I also got into trouble in most of my classes for talking too much to all the new friends and my life-long buddies from Lincoln. Mischief found me, and I welcomed it, especially whenever friends were involved. Most of the time I was lucky enough to avoid teacher-sanctioned visits to the office for a chat with our principal there, Charlie Stidwell.

One of the more memorable classroom experiences that year came when Billy Freudenthal did something to irritate our English teacher, Mrs. Weaver. This was nothing new. Billy was good at that. However, on that particular day, he mastered the skill of irritating Mrs. Weaver so completely that she hauled off and hit him over the head with a plastic ruler. As the yellow plastic fragments dribbled down the sides of his head, Billy simply giggled and scrunched his shoulders up around his neck to avoid any further assaults from the ruler. The rest of the class sat back and watched, muffling any hints of sadistic amusement. News of such incidents traveled through school hallways like lightning. With our introduction to the world of adolescence came the need to gossip and marvel at the naughty little things that happened in our day-to-day adjustment to the new school.

The drama that accompanied the novelty of junior high caused the fall to pass quickly. By Christmas vacation, the whole family was getting excited about the arrival of our new brother or sister. We had to wait almost the entire vacation and just about saw 1959 pass away. Finally Mother and Harold decided that the baby's time had come, and left for the hospital to meet with Dr. Hayden, the same doctor who had delivered me.

As we kids sat and watched our favorite TV programs that night, we could hardly concentrate. A beaming Harold returned just after midnight, December 31, to tell us our new little sister was "half-grown." "She looks like a little Eskimo baby," he told us. "She has a full head of black hair." Harold was obviously tickled with his new daughter. Barbara Iva Tibbs weighed nine pounds, seven ounces when she was born.

We couldn't wait for Mother to bring her home, but three days passed before the Ford Ranchwagon rolled in to the driveway and Harold got out to help Mother carry the new bundle into the house. "Okay, Punkin, here's your new home," she said while gently placing Barbara in her bassinet. Three adoring teenagers surrounded the miniature bed and gazed proudly at their new little sister. Mother never had a shortage of hands willing to hold, rock, or feed Barbara, who was indeed a beautiful baby with three inches of coal black hair, an almond complexion, and huge charcoal gray eyes. We learned to change diapers, make formula, and bathe our baby sister. Kevin turned out to be the best babysitter; he seemed to have the secret touch while rocking Barbara back and forth on his lap.

With a healthy wardrobe of pretty little dresses, Barbara became the favored subject for Mother's camera. Over a few short years the family photograph topic had evolved from Montana deer to North Boyer horses to a pretty little baby. Our new little sister also dominated much of our time in the living room every afternoon when we came home from school.

Joanne Buhr's little sister was born after Barbara, in 1960—a leap year. Joanne and I often compared notes about the two babies. Our seventh-grade crowd walked the halls, perfected our gossip skills, gawked at boys, and planned gatherings designed for even more fun outside of school—slumber parties. At the end of the year, we held our first overnighter at Judy Turnbull's house in the country near Sagle, about five miles south of Sandpoint. A dozen or so attended. Some of us didn't get any sleep, and those who wanted to sleep got mad. Neither situation, however, dampened anyone's desire to plan future slumber parties for our social calendar. We perfected them over the years so that the sleep-to-devilishness ratio averaged about one to ten. Party-poopers who chose to sleep rather than play growled in the early morning hours at the humiliation of having to retrieve pilfered bras from the Northern Lights power-pole guy wires as passersby pointed and guffawed at the sight.

By eighth grade, we had our daily routine down and our groups firmly established. We all attended the SJHS Bullpup athletic events and screamed our lungs out for sports stars such as Smokey Chubb and Mike Parkins. I attended lots of Pep Club meetings and wrote homeroom reports for the school's mimeographed newspaper.

Meanwhile, at home, Barbara was learning to walk—and Mother was putting on some weight around the middle again. Having become knowledgeable about such things, we pretty much figured out what was happening, but nobody said anything until one day when her close friend Helen Crockett came to the house and decided to satisfy her curiosity. "Are you expecting again?" she asked Mother. Sure enough she was, and soon. We were all so busy with our school activities that the boys and I didn't call a conference on this one.

Laurie's birth on Saturday, April 7, 1961, coincided with my invitation to another fun-filled slumber party at Joanne Buhr's house. However, after learning about our new little sister, I called Joanne and told her I would not be able to make it to her party. It was tough to have to bypass the party, but I knew that my help was expected around the house.

We all welcomed Laurie and fell in love with her immediately. She was very different from Barbara—no hair, fair skin, and blue eyes. In fact, her blonde hair remained pretty scant until she was about a year old. We nicknamed her "Willie Wirehead" after the bald mascot for a local power company. Years later, during her teen-age days, Laurie was convinced she was adopted because she still looked so different from the rest of us. Mother eventually had to produce a birth certificate to allay her concerns.

The pleasures of having two little sisters were beyond my wildest dreams. They were a bit young to tag along with me but I looked forward to future years when they would become my friends. Our family life had definitely taken on a whole new dimension as the little girls kept everyone in the family entertained. A new bedroom and porch were added to the house. The group at the kitchen-table expanded as high chairs edged their way into the vacant spots. After-dinner conversations continued along the same vein as they had for years, occasionally interrupted by little folks playing with their peas or blowing bubbles with their spit.

During the year after Laurie was born, we began facing the prospects of another change in our family unit. Mike was a senior looking toward college. Having been fully involved as a 4-H member, honor student, athlete, and class leader, he had assembled an impressive list of achievements. Everybody ex-

pected Mike to go to the University of Idaho, major in agricul-
ture, and become a farmer. Mike had other ideas. He had inves-
tigated the possibility of attending a service academy and had
started taking the necessary tests necessary and contacting
elected officials during his junior year.

We were all excited about this possibility, especially me; it
was hard to believe that anyone from our family could ever
achieve such an honor. In May, after receiving nominations from
Representative Gracie Pfost and Senator Frank Church, Mike
learned that he would definitely be attending the United States
Military Academy at West Point.

His good fortune helped Mother and Harold avoid the worry
of where to get the money for his higher education. From the
time we were little kids we knew we would be going to college
somehow, regardless of cost. It was considered the next phase of
our education. The only question was "how" and "where." Mike
was aware of this. Besides having access to one of the finest
educations available, attending the academy would ease the
burden on his parents.

He graduated from Sandpoint High School in 1962. A month
later he had to depart by train for New York to enroll in the
academy. Barbara and Laurie stayed with a babysitter, while
the rest of us took another family drive in the Ford ranchwagon
to the train depot in Spokane, Washington, about eighty-five
miles away.

When we left town, Mike's friends formed a caravan and
followed us across the bridge, all the time honking their good-
byes. At 11 P.M. that June evening we said good-bye to our big
brother in the darkness, knowing we would not see him again
for almost a year because at the time the academy did not allow
its plebes to come home for Christmas. He boarded the train
and went off into the night. We sobbed all the way home and for
three days afterward wandered around numb, as if someone

had died. Our apple cart had been upset one more time.

It took a long time to adjust to Mike's absence, but Kevin and I found a new relationship that summer as sister and brother. He had gotten to know my friend Susie Baldwin, who lived about half a mile down the road. The three of us entertained ourselves by planning adventures to caves, the creek, and other neighborhood attractions such as newly vacated houses. I dare not disclose the specifics of our activities, except to say that I often came home with battle scars—ripped up pants and mucky shoes that had not survived the slides down rocky hillsides or the sprints through foot-deep mud in the wetlands alongside Sand Creek. The illicit evening adventures throughout the countryside had blended our unit into one of the tightest trios around.

Then summer ended, and Kevin and I both went to high school. On my first day I saw him in the hall at noon and greeted him with what I thought was a pretty friendly "Hello." My mortal sin became perfectly clear as we walked home from our bus stop after school. "Don't you ever talk to me at school again!" he ordered. "Don't say one word to me." His tone convinced me of the importance of schizophrenic brother-sister relationships. I knew my place throughout the remaining years of high school. From that day forward, I dutifully assumed the role of anonymous sister by day and trusted confidante by night.

During my junior year Joanne Buhr, babies, and slumber parties found common ground once more. By that time, Mike had finished a year at West Point and Kevin was a first-stringer on the high school football team. As the little girls were starting to discover the barnyard, cows, and horses, Mother and Harold were quietly looking toward one more addition to Batch Two.

Football was the name of the game that year at Sandpoint High School. The whole town was following the Bulldogs as they trounced team after team. Mother become an avid football fan because Kevin was having such a good year. One of the toughest tests for the team would be the Lewiston game, which also happened to be Homecoming. Joanne Buhr again invited me to a slumber party, that Friday night. We planned to go to the game and then head for her house afterward, and I looked forward to the weekend with great anticipation. Even Mother and Harold planned to go to the game to watch Kevin.

The best-laid plans of the Tibbs family fell through early that night when Mother started having labor pains. Kevin had already left for the game. Concerned that Dr. Hayden, a Bulldog fan, might have left also, Harold called and alerted him. The doctor decided to bring his radio along to the delivery room so he could at least listen to the game. In the meantime, somebody had to stay home to babysit. "Somebody" was me. "Joanne will not believe this," I thought as I dialed her number.

"Hello?"

"Joanne, this is Marianne. I'm afraid I can't come to your party. My mother is at the hospital having a baby."

Momentary silence was followed by skeptical giggle. "Come on, you can't use that for an excuse; you've already used it," she insisted.

"No, it's true," I assured Joanne. "She just headed for the hospital to have a baby."

My perennial slumber party hostess remained incredulous until she saw the proof a day or so later. But if she ever had any more slumber parties, she didn't invite me.

My little brother Jim came screaming into the world at half-time of the Lewiston-Sandpoint football game. Mother and Dr. Hayden listened as the Bulldogs kept their winning streak alive with a nine-to-seven thriller. Kevin helped score the two-point safety that won the game. His team went undefeated, a record not matched for at least thirty years thereafter. Batch Two was now complete. Two little sisters and one little brother rounded out the Tibbs kids. The house was full, and it would be Christmas before Mike would meet his new little brother, twenty years his junior.

As they grew into independent little farm girls, Barbara and Laurie became a team of animal trainers—horses, cows, cats, they would train anything that was alive, even an occasional frog. At the tender ages of three and four, they were horrifying neighbors who would drive by and spot them swinging from one of the horse's tails in the front pasture. They also spent lots of time in the barnyard grooming the cows. Mother's efforts to create porcelain dolls for daughters failed once more.

Jim, on the other hand, took his time acquiring the family's love for horses. A bit of a loner, he walked to a different drum than his older sisters. This was especially evident one day when he set off on a journey across the pasture. We were all visiting near the gate that led to the field at the time. About four years old, Jim was wearing one of Harold's western hats. The hat was almost bigger than he was. As we watched him leave the barnyard and amble off down the well-beaten trail, the herd of five horses started coming toward the barn on the same path. Jim kept walking as the horses got closer and closer, and neither party volunteered to get off the path. When kid and horses were just a few feet from decision time, Jim finally gave in to the first horse and grudgingly stepped to the side. "Damn horse," he said, unaware that anyone was watching or listening.

He met face to face with the second horse, eventually having to move aside once more. "Damn horse," he muttered again.

The third horse came. Jim stepped aside. "Damn horse," he repeated.

Again and again, the little boy with the huge hat stepped aside to let the horses pass—five "damn" horses in all.

His opinion of the equine species did change eventually. Years later he, like Barbara and Laurie, became an accomplished horseman in the local 4-H circles. Unaware that the horses really meant much to Jim, one night the folks sat at the kitchen table and talked of selling his Appaloosa mare Tonka. After overhearing the conversation, Jim abruptly disappeared and was gone for several hours before the whole family began combing the woods and the neighborhood searching for him. He finally reappeared late that evening, dejected and visibly upset. It was then that we learned how much he really loved the "damn" horses. After hearing Mother and Harold's conversation, he had decided to leave home. So he climbed Greenhorn Mountain behind the house, sat and thought for a while, then decided he might as well come back. Jim's old mare never left the place; she's buried among the cedar trees in the woods along with all the other horse friends we loved through the years.

All three members of Batch Two found their niche on the family farm and occupied their days with projects which foreshadowed their adult lives. While the girls tended to barnyard projects or rode imaginary horses through the woods, Jim created an elaborate miniature city, complete with power lines and parking lots, in his sand pile behind the house.

As Batch One gradually phased out of life on the farm and found futures of their own, a much tamer, less impish Batch Two was beginning to roam the fields, ride the horses, and heckle new generations of cows on the North Boyer farm.

GOOD-BYE *to the*
North IDAHO FARM

After Batch Two was complete, and after Kevin left for college, I spent one year being the oldest kid in the family. My senior year was a busy one. I had taken on some leadership responsibilities at school, including the vice presidency of Pep Club and projects chairman for the Senior Class. The pride of my life, however, was serving as editor of the *Cedar Post* newspaper.

My journalism teacher Bob Hamilton opened the door for me when he took me aside one day and told me I had the talent to become a pretty fair journalist. That spring he had added to the claim by offering my the editorship of the paper. Up to that moment, I 'd spent most of my life feeling like an average klutz who could only accomplish mediocre feats.

I had always wanted to be good at something because I was surrounded by so many talented friends and family members. My track record so far had been pretty average, but Mr. Hamilton changed that. He was my mentor. I admired him and listened to every word he said about journalism, determined that I would spend my life as a journalist or teacher. I wanted to go to my mother's alma mater in Kalamazoo, Michigan, and even took some of the initial steps to enroll there. If accepted, I would live with my Aunt Louise and help earn my way by getting a job at Upjohn Pharmaceuticals, where Harold's cousin worked as a researcher.

As decision time approached I knew we didn't have the money, and I also thought that two thousand miles was too far away from the cows, horse, and family that I loved. I ended up deciding to attend the University of Idaho in Moscow. After receiving my financial aid application, the school offered me one of the first ever positions in its work-study program. My classmate Terry Chronic and I would spend three weeks working at the Radio-TV Center in Moscow and the rest of the summer washing dishes at Camp Neewahlu for Campfire girls on Lake Coeur d'Alene. My college plans were set by late March. All I had to do was finish my senior year and graduate. Like most seniors, I turned into an arrogant know-it-all during the last few months of school.

Toward the end of the year we could hear the orchestra practicing "Pomp and Circumstance" every day from the journalism room. Whenever they sounded the first note my friend Barbara Kitt broke into uncontrollable sobs. She could not handle the thought that we would soon be going our separate ways, in some cases never to meet again. Some were headed to college, while others would find themselves in Vietnam instead as military recruits. My friend Glen Shropshire, author of the class prophecy section for the *Cedar Post* senior edition, was joining the Marines. Barbara's fears came true a few short years later when Glen was killed in action.

When our class of 194 students graduated as the largest ever in Sandpoint High history, we did what most high school graduates do—we counted the dollars that friends and relatives sent us for graduation. As we marched in our red and white caps and gowns, we tried to spot family members in the over-flowing gym. We didn't listen too closely to the guest speaker, and just before Marian Ruyle's orchestra played the "Alma Mater," Barbara started her sobs.

Afterward, Laura Delmarter, her boyfriend Lee, and my recruited date Ray Holt and I thumbed our noses at the Elks graduation party and headed for Spokane for a big night on the town. We decided to go to the Ridpath and dine at its fine restaurant, but when we arrived about 11 P.M., we were shocked to find it closed. They apparently hadn't heard we were coming. We ended up eating at Smitty's Pancake House on Sprague Avenue. The metal table wobbled back and forth as we stabbed bites of bacon and hot cakes and talked about nothing. We drove back to Sandpoint in silence. I was in bed by 2 A.M.

Two days later, I had to pack my belongings for the move to Moscow. Mother was busy with the three little kids who were beginning to scout our their territory outside their house and around the barnyard. One era on the farm was passing, another beginning. I spent the whole day making decisions on what to leave and what to take. That evening I went down to the Baldwins to say good-bye to my friend Susie. The Baldwins, too, would soon move away.

The next morning I rose early and wandered around the farm—Mother and Harold's dream and my home for fifteen years. I took one last trip through the field to scratch the cows, including Millie, the subject of virtually every one of my essays in Mary Parker's class.

I spent lots of time talking to and petting each of the horses' muzzles while sitting on the granary step. Etching the images of my barnyard friends in my mind, I headed for the house to eat a last piece of toast and jam at the table where my life had been molded. Harold ate his Wheaties breakfast cereal, still loaded with a mountain of sugar and cream. Mother drank her black coffee and finished off a piece of toast before getting dressed for the three-hour drive to Moscow. A few last words of advice from both of them, and I headed to my room to get the suitcases and load them in the car. The luggage sat in the middle of an empty bedroom. The pictures were down, the dresser bare except for a decorative mirror Mother had given me for Christmas a few years before.

It was time to leave the place where my parents had taught me honesty, good manners, responsibility, pride in work, loyalty, and fairness. I was armed with the tools to seek my dreams and lead a good life. Now I had to use my own initiative to make it all work during the years ahead. I had to go, but I knew I could always come back for their advice and roam the fields that had fed my fantasies and protected me from the world I have yet to greet.

I stood motionless and gazed in the mirror as a huge lump formed in my throat and tears welled up in my eyes. "It's over," I thought. "It'll never be the same again, but it sure was fun." Then I dried my eyes, composed myself, and left the room to start a new chapter in my life.

That fall I started my college career at the University of Idaho, where thirteen Sandpoint girls helped initiate a brand new dorm on campus. It was a tough year because I worked fifteen hours a week in the university's first work-study program. My tendency to be the hall prankster and informal social director, along with the work load, had a severe effect on my efforts to perform as the model student. As a junior I moved off campus, away from the temptations that frequently kept me away from my books. My grade point improved enough that I can almost bear to share it with close friends.

I worked four summers with the U.S.D.A. Forest Service

as a traffic surveyor. Besides the lookouts, my partner Sis Ballenger and I were among the first females to work in the field. Christine Moon, another SHS grad, joined me the last two years. The combination produced some good stories during the daily coffee breaks. We learned to drive some narrow, rugged mountain roads, remaining ever vigilant for the dreaded roar of a loaded logging truck, which meant backing the "rig" a mile or two down the hillside. Chris and I also took our share of spontaneous, unsanctioned adventures in our Dodge Powerwagon, a noisy, dented-up bucket of bolts that had been rejected by the Job Corps. We always had a plausible story ready in case our supervisors learned that we'd been driving the streets of some Canadian border town.

After completing a successful student teaching experience at my alma mater, I began my career as an English teacher and yearbook adviser at Sandpoint High School. Twenty-five years and about three thousand students later, I still teach at Sandpoint High School. I began advising the *Cedar Post* newspaper after Bob Hamilton retired in 1990.

In 1974 my students had to quit calling me Miss Brown because I married Bill Love, a native of Oakdale, Louisiana. He now works as the bureau chief for private forestry in the Idaho Department of Lands in Coeur d'Alene. He plays golf, plays golf, and plays some more golf—and puts up with me.

We live on almost ten acres about a mile from my childhood home, and we have two and one-twelfth children—Willie (or William, as he prefers), Annie, and our French honorary son from Caen who spends one month with us each summer. Willie (as I prefer to call him) loves sports, admires Michael Jordan, video tapes local sporting events and weddings, and envisions the day when he will be President of the United States. He has been a student leader throughout his high school career. Annie likes to do crafts, plays on the high school golf team, does well with horsemanship, admires Michael Jordan, and loves to get organized and plan ahead. She's always had executive qualities, and she envisions herself going to a large Eastern university.

Besides our kids we care for two horses, two dogs that don't stay home, and several inbred black cats known as The Blacks. We also raise snowdrifts in our driveway during the winter and grow twine in the barnyard all year long. During the ruthless winter of 1993, our place was a tourist stop for locals eager to see just how much snow could be packed into one spot. One neighbor even called anonymously with a thinly veiled threat. "All right. It's okay for you to grow snowdrifts," he said, "but we'd all appreciate it if you'd keep them inside your fence and off the road."

Our twine yield usually depends on just how deep the mud gets in the barnyard during the spring. When and if it ever dries out, the orange loops begin popping up all over the barnyard. I usually pull most of them but have to resort to scissors to harvest the more stubborn strings.

When the wind isn't blowing the sides off the machine shed, the building provides a nice shelter for our dead lawnmowers. Briggs and Stratton hasn't yet mastered a machine sturdy enough to mow rocks, and I haven't figured out how to dodge the stones while cutting the weeds along the ditch.

It's a good life here on our 1990s farm. Here are more updates:

VIRGINIA HALTER TIBBS: My mother works one or two days a week at the Country Loft in Foster's Crossing Antique Mall in Sandpoint, where she markets her cards. She also sells them at local and regional crafts fairs. She attended her fiftieth college reunion in Michigan in the fall of 1992.

Mother's pride-and-joy includes her husband, six kids, five

grandkids, horses, garden, dog Chukker, and herd of cats. She allows the family to tease her about losing forty percent of her hearing but refuses to purchase a hearing aid.

She recently completed radiation treatments in Coeur d'Alene after surgery to remove a cancerous polyp. As always, humor has helped her through the ordeal. She claimed to have the worst sunburn in the worst possible place on her body. "Anyone who has it anywhere else doesn't have to sit on it," she lamented.

Now in her early seventies, Mother still has lots of spunk, and knows how to bang the pots and pans in the cupboard really loud when she's mad at some member of the family.

HAROLD TIBBS: Harold retired from the water department in the early 1980s. Since then, he has devoted most of his time to the daily needs of the farm, which include everything from feeding to haying to fixing fences. Harold still tells stories about his experiences in Montana. Everyone who listens to his tales says we need to write a book about his life.

The family had a scare in 1981 when, at sixty-five, he started losing his interest in food and began to fade away to almost a skeleton. His mysterious ailment could not be detected for almost eight months. Harold, who normally weighs about 165 pounds, had lost 65 and eventually couldn't do anything for himself. Finally, the doctors determined that he was suffering from Addison's Disease, a malady that affects the pituitary gland. The body quits producing cortisone and gets completely out of whack.

Once he started taking cortisone pills Harold went through a miraculous recovery, which has allowed him to have a second chance at life. He hasn't wasted the opportunity.

MIKE BROWN: Mike graduated from West Point in 1966

as a member of the class featured in Washington Post writer Rick Atkinson's book *The Long Gray Line*. He served twice in Vietnam, first through the Tet Offensive and again in 1972 when his Cobra helicopter was shot down by a surface to air missile (SAM). He received recognition in *Stars and Stripes* newspaper and *Aviation Digest* as the first American pilot to survive being hit by a SAM missile. After crash landing his helicopter in a Vietnamese bunker, Mike suffered only a minor scratch on his finger when he broke open the door to escape. He was rescued a few minutes later. He resigned from the Army after returning from Vietnam. Since that time, he has worked in the paper industry in the United States, Mexico, Thailand, and Venezuela. If he ever chooses to abandon his career he can work as a double for Sean Connery.

Mike married his high school classmate and friend Mary Thompson in 1967. She teaches Fortune 500 employees writing and English skills. Their older daughter Maureen works as a counselor at a residential mental health facility in Tacoma, Washington. She recently married Sean Peterson, a fellow Pacific Lutheran University graduate from Olympia, Washington. Mike and Mary's younger daughter Laura attends Cornell University, where she is majoring in pre-veterinary studies.

KEVIN BROWN: After working summers in white pine blister rust control for the U.S.D.A. Forest Service, Kevin moved to Missoula, Montana, where he joined the Forest Service smokejumpers. As a jumper, he bailed into back country throughout the Western states and Alaska. On his fiftieth jump, his chute caught in the top of a tree. Kevin broke both ankles in the fall and said good-bye to jumping. He has continued to work for the Forest Service in the Missoula area as a fire specialist.

In 1968, Kevin married Joyce Dahm, whom he met while working winters on the ski patrol at Schweitzer Mountain Resort in Sandpoint. Joyce now teaches at Clinton Elementary School east of Missoula, where she specializes in the gifted and talented program. Their son Scott attends the University of Montana, where he has played for the Grizzly football team.

BARBARA TIBBS: Earning a 4.0 GPA, Barbara finished high school as valedictorian of her class in 1978. She earned a degree in English from the College of Education at the University of Idaho, where she graduated with honors. Barbara teaches English, photography, and yearbook at Sandpoint High School. She also gives riding lessons to adults and kids at the family farm on North Boyer. For several years she has worked with aspiring young horse judges who have earned several national awards under her tutelage. During the summers, Barbara and Laurie travel around the region showing their Arabian horses.

LAURIE TIBBS: Barbara and Laurie have worked as a team throughout their lives. After graduating from Sandpoint High School in 1979, Laurie attended the University of Idaho and earned her elementary education degree in less than four years. She received special honors from the College of Education. While attending the university, both sisters took dressage lessons from Olympic equestrian instructor Betty Tukey. With her extensive horse knowledge, hours of hard work and riding ability, Laurie trained and rode a gelding named Rishmah to the U.S. Arabian National Top Ten award in Show Hack in 1987. She teaches fifth grade at Farmin Elementary School in Sandpoint.

JIM TIBBS: We've always teased Mother about Jim being her favorite. He's the youngest of the half dozen, and he inherited her artistic talent. Jim lives outside of Kalispell, Montana, where he works as an architect. He too graduated from the

University of Idaho. He has followed in Mother's footsteps by marketing pen and ink notecards. His most recent series features the lodges of Montana's Glacier National Park. His work has also appeared on the back cover of *Whitefish Magazine.*

Jim's wife Julie (Schauer), whom he married in 1992, works for the Credit Bureau of Kalispell.

THE NORTH BOYER FARM: The original forty-acre farm expanded to ninety-five acres in 1966 when Mother and Harold purchased the adjoining Harney Dairy. They have since sold a small plot that runs along Great Northern Road and have become battle-weary after more than two decades of dealing with the local airport and problems of land acquisition and air rights. When Mother first purchased the property in 1950, Sandpoint's airstrip ran east and west about half a mile south of the place. Now, it extends to the northeast across what was once Boyer and my folks' front hayfield. Lear jets coming in and out of Sandpoint frequently take off about two hundred feet from their house. My sisters continue to give their riding lessons and train their horses in the front pasture. The horses have learned to ignore the jets.

SANDPOINT: My home town has changed considerably over the years. After the hubbub of World War II and the closing of Farragut Naval Training Base, Sandpoint reverted to a quiet farming and logging community which went into virtual hibernation every year from Labor Day to the beginning of summer. That isolation ceased in 1964 with the initial development of Schweitzer Mountain Resort. Along with the avalanche of skiers came real estate companies, land developers, restaurants, and motels. As the ski area continued to grow, more and more outsiders "discovered" Sandpoint and decided to grab a little piece of heaven along or near the shores of Lake Pend Oreille.

The North Idaho area has, over the past decade, attracted a wide crosssection of new inhabitants, each seeking their own brand of getaway from the outside world. The combination leads to never-ending dialogue.

We are home to the Festival at Sandpoint, which annually attracts some of the finest musical talent in the world. Our Love family enjoys volunteering for the three-week festival every summer, where thousands of residents and visitors flock with their picnics to enjoy everything from old-time country western music to contemporary classics night after night. Meanwhile, when Timberfest rolls around every summer, scores of loggers and locals appear from behind every tree to re-acknowledge the importance of their outdoor industry. Many of the farms are gone, but the county fair still attracts folks from miles around who like to stand around and talk about what's happened since the last time they saw each other the year before. Logging trucks, cement mixers, loud cars, and portable storage units still tend to be the crowd pleasers in the annual Fourth of July Parade.

Sandpoint has changed a lot from the place I knew as a child. I seriously doubt that I could get away with some of the exploits of my inventive youth if I were growing up in my home town these days. I'd be in jail.

ILLUSTRATIONS

by Virginia and Jim Tibbs

Cover–Marianne, Kevin, Mike, and Bossy the Guernsey milkcow.

Introduction—Winter scene on Sand Creek at the old Schweitzer Mountain Resort road.

Bless me, Father, for I Have Sinned—St. Joseph's Catholic Church, our parish church on Oak Street in Sandpoint.

Great Pencil Mystery—Mother on her beloved half-Arabian mare Cricket.

Instant Kids—Harold on his Appaloosa stallion Toby I. With his registration number 203, Toby was one of the foundation sires listed in the Appaloosa Horse Club registry.

Used Car, Abused Car Blues—Boy driving a Belgian draft horse. Sketch by Jim Tibbs.

Sunday Gambles—Gate scene near Hamilton, Montana

Great Horned Cows—Millie, my great horned Hereford, and one of her bull calves.

Foot Cover-Ups that Failed—Marianne at about six years of age.

Why Mother's Cupboard Went Bare—Appaloosas during winter, with the Tibbs house in the background.

Pocket Girdles—Mother's childhood home, the Douglas mansion in Manistee, Michigan.

The Nuts and Bolts of Junior High School Choir—Wagon wheel in winter near Sandpoint.

Kids, Dogs, Cows, etc.—Idaho Draft Horse International Show, held every October in Sandpoint

They Took the Cake—Love's Barn.

Smoke, Smoke, Smoke that Cigarette—Harold and his own cigarette.

Good & Plentys Won't Getcha Love—Mother and Harold in a sleigh.

Marianne's Left-Handed Approach to Life—Mother riding Largo and me slip-sliding away on Darkie.

Batch Two—Jim on the trail.

Good-bye to the North Idaho Farm—Barbara, Laurie, and Millie.

For more information about pen and ink sketches and notecards by Virginia Tibbs or Jim Tibbs, write:

Virginia Tibbs
Greenhorn Mountain Notecards
110 Center Valley Road
Sandpoint, Idaho 83864
(208) 263-3308

Jim Tibbs
Legacy Press
220 Gilbert Lake Drive
Kalispell, Montana 59901
(406) 755-5022

ABOUT THE AUTHOR

Photo by Annie Love.

If Marianne Love didn't have a sense of humor, she'd never have lasted so long in North Idaho. With words at hand, she has persevered, teaching English and Journalism at Sandpoint High School since 1969. Thanks to her, generations of students now appreciate everyday hilarity.

A graduate of the University of Idaho, Moscow, Love has written over the years for Spokane's *Spokesman-Review*, the *Idaho Register, North Idaho Sunday*, the *Spokane Daily Chronicle*, and the *Sandpoint News Bulletin*. Her work with high school journalists has earned regional acclaim and the Dow Jones Newspaper Fund's national award as "Special Recognized High School Journalism Teacher," among other honors.

A local horse show announcer, emcee, Festival volunteer, horse fanatic, and dog owner, Love lives in Sandpoint with her husband Bill and their children, William and Annie.

You just read everything else you need to know.